THE

SANDHYAVANDANAM

OF

Rig. Yajus and Sama Vedins

WITH

a literal translation an explanatory paraphrase

&

Commentary in English

THE

SANDHYAVANDANAM

OF

Rig Yajus and Sama Vedins

WITH

a literal translation an explanatory paraphrase

And

Commentary in English

BY

B.V. KAMESVARA AIYAR M.A.

Professor of English. H.H. The Maha Raja's College of Pudukottai

&

Editor, Sanskrit Journal.

KALPAZ

ISBN: 978-93-5128-762-9(PB)

First Published in 1808
Indian Reprint in 2017

Published by

Kalpaz Publications
C-30, Satyawati Nagar,
Delhi – 110052
E-mail: kalpaz@hotmail.com
Website: kalpazpublications.com
Ph.: +91-9212142040

SANDHYAVANDANAM.

Introduction.

Sandhyâvandanam is the daily prayer of the Aryans of India. It is a noble institution embodying a simple faith and breathing a lofty spirituality. And yet most of us Brahmans have turned it into a farce more or less. We have no time for it in these busy days. We hardly suspect its existence till it is time for breakfast or dinner; then *mâmûl* steps in and rudely reminds us of a duty we owe to Brahmanhood. We throw down a few spoonfuls of water and utter a few words which convey no meaning to us and feel satisfied that we have discharged a debt that is due to our religion. We fail to see that here as elsewhere the letter killeth, but the spirit giveth life.

We had better not do a thing than do

it in this perfunctory manner. Let us see if it is worth doing and if it is worth the trouble let us do it well. How can we hope to catch the spirit of the prayer when we have no idea of what it means? Yet most of us have not the slightest idea of what is meant by the several *Mantras* we recite. Our *Sâstras* lay down that it is useless, if not mischievous, to recite the *Mantras* without a knowledge of their meaning. Such a course is compared to threshing chaff instead of threshing the corn,—तुषाणांखण्डनंयथा. It has been said :

स्थाणुरयं भारहारः किलाभूत्
अधीत्यवेदं न विजानाति योर्थम् ।
योऽर्थज्ञइत्सकलं भद्रमश्नुते
नाकमेति ज्ञानविधूतपाप्मा ॥

He who learning the Vedas by rote does not know their meaning is a mere block of wood, a mere carrier of burdens.

He who knows the meaning is absolved, through his knowledge, of all his sins, enjoys all happiness, and (at last) goes to heaven. अनर्थज्ञ or he who does not know the meaning is counted among the six kinds of पाठकाधम—'the worst of reciters.' So also says the *Chhândogya S'ruti:*

तेनोभौ कुरुतो यश्चैतदेवंवेद
यश्चनवेद । नानातु विद्या चाविद्याच ।
यदेव विद्यया करोति श्रद्धया
उपनिषदा तदेव वीर्यवत्तरं भवति ।

'Both do this, he who knows and he who does not know; knowing and not knowing are different things. That which one does with knowledge, with faith and wisdom, that alone becomes efficacious.'

In the face of texts like these many of our orthodox countrymen would regard an equiry into the meaning of the Scriptures a profanation. What a pity!

The *Sandhyâ* service is binding on all.

All the *smritis* and Purânas dwell on its necessity. Vidyâranya, in his commentary on *Parâsara Smriti*, brings together some of the authorities bearing on this point. A free translation of the passage is given below.

Vyâsa says that Sandhyâ is the prayer to God that we offer in the morning and the evening twilight. *Yâjnavalkya* says that we should perform this service thrice a day, before the sun sinks entirely below the horizon, before the sun has entirely risen above the horizon, and at midday. The Scriptures (Taitt. Aran. II Pra, 2 anu) state that the Brahman who meditates on the rising and the setting sun as the Supreme being enjoys all happiness. The *Vishnu Purâna* states that those who do not perform the *Sandhyâ* service are sent to the dark hell, and *Gôbhila* says in his *smriti* that one who neglects the *Sandhyâ* becomes a *sûdra* while living and is born a dog after death. *Yâjnavalkya* declares in his *Smriti* that he who omits the *Sandhya*, in the absence of sufficient reason such as illness, comes to ruin; and *Pulastyâ* lays down that the service should be gone through even in times of pollution.

The *Dharma sûtras* lay down a similar injunction. Gautama, for instance, says: 'And the morning and evening devotions —*Sandhyâ*—must be performed outside the village. Silent he shall stand during the former and sit during the latter from the time when one light is still visible until the other light appears (Gautama) II, 10 & 11; also compare Apastamba I, 11, 30, 8.)

In the Râmâyana and the Mahâ-Bhârata frequent mention is made of the service and we read how scrupulously *Râma*, *Yudhishthira* and others went through the ceremony even in times of emergency.

A text is often quoted from the Scriptures laying down the imperative nature of this duty. 'अहरहः सन्ध्यामुपासीत' 'worship the *Sandhyâ* every day'. There is an *arthavâda* on the subject in the *Taittiriya Aranyaka*, (II Prapathaka, 2nd anuvâka), a free translation of which is given below.

"In former days the evil spirits performed a severe penance. *Prajâpati* granted them a boon. They made this request—that the sun should consent to fight with them. *Prajâpati* said to them 'Fight on'. And so the evil spirits fight with the rising sun till he sets; and these evil spirits are vanquished by the water consecrated by the *Gâyatrî*.

'Therefore it is that the wise *Brahmavâdins* in this world face the east during the morning twilight and throw up water consecrated by the *Gâyatrî*. These waters becoming thunderbolts hurl the evil spirits to an island called *Aruna* where dwell the evil spirits called *Mandehas*.

'These *Brahmavâdins* then perform a circumambulation around themselves. By this they scatter away their sins.

'The Brahman who knowing that the sun is the same as the Supreme Brahman meditates on the rising and the setting sun and then performs a circumambulation enjoys all happiness.

'He who knows this (*i. e.*, the secret of this identity) is himself Brahman and attains Brahman.'

These quotations will also serve to show that this institution of *Sandhya* has been in existence from very early times.

Sandhyâvandanam is essentially a Vedic prayer. We find in it many verses in the later style as it is now recited among us. But these are the additions of a later age and are due to the sectarian, *purânic*, and other influences brought to bear on our practice from time to time. In the following pages an attempt is made to give a literal meaning of the several vedic texts used in the service and offer such comments as may be suggested by them.

'*Sandhya*' means 'the time when day and night meet and '*Vandanam*' means 'thanksgiving', so that the expression '*Sandhyâvandanam*' means the prayer of thanksgiving to God during the morning and the evening twilight. Sir Monier Williams would explain *Sandhyâ* to mean a prayer well meditated on (from सं well and ध्यै to meditate upon). But this explanation ignores the importance to be attached to the time when the service should be performed.... The analogy of the term *Mâdhyâhnika* (the service during mid-day) favours the orthodox derivation.

It may be asked that if Sandhya is nothing but a prayer to the Almighty it is reasonable to pray in the language which we daily use. Our reply is this. We believe that the blood of sages—Rishis that lived more than 4,000 years ago—runs in our veins. We have a distinguished ancestry to be proud of—an ancestry that goes back to a period of time earlier than any that any modern nation can claim. It gratifies our feelings of nationality to think that the prayer we now utter is in fact the very one which was uttered by our ancestors thousands of years ago. All this, apart from the intrinsic worth of the language in which our prayer is couched, its ability to express the nicest shades of meaning, the sublime character of the prayer in question, and the value to be attached to the associations of Vedic simplicity and Vedic Poetry which it is calculated to recall.

It is interesting in this connection to note how our Sandhyâ service strikes a sympathetic *Christian* Sanskritist like Sir Monier Williams. He says (in his Brahmanism and Hinduism):

"We are so accustomed to give all our attention to the Veda for purely literary or philological objects that we are apt to forget that, directly or indirectly, for good or for evil, these ancient books—the oldest in the world except, *perhaps*, portions of the Christian Bible—have for three thousand years moulded the faith, inspired the prayers, animated the aspirations, influenced the conduct, shaped the lives of a large portion of the great Aryan race to which we ourselves belong. And to this very day the remarkable spectacle may be seen of millions of Indo-Aryans, comprising countless tribes of various origin, scattered over a vast area from the Punjab to Cape Comorin, from Bombay to Assam, living distinct from each other in separate castes and communities, yet all *united by the common bond of this Veda, which they still use as their daily prayer-Book."*

A Brâhman should rise early in the morning (in what is called Brâhma Muhûrta *i.e.*, the hour and a half that immediately precede sun-rise), go out (preferably a few furlongs to the west of his residence) and clean his teeth. He should then bathe in some sacred stream, but in default of a river he may use a pool or tank. He should then mark his forehead and some other parts of his body with the sacred marks* of his own faith.

First comes *Achamana* (आचमन or sipping water). A little water is taken in the palm of the right hand, just sufficient to moisten a grain of pulse माष and sipped. This is done three times, after this nine parts

---

* A Siva-worshipper rubs ashes on the head, the forehead, across the breast, the navel and the elbow joints. The ashes used should, strictly speaking, be taken from the औपासनाग्नि (the sacred domestic

of the body are touched. The water sipped is supposed to cleanse the internal parts of the body in its downward course, just in the same way as bathing cleanses the external parts of the body. Achamana is a purificatory act and is the usual preliminary to all Hindu religious rites.

It was a simple thing at first, but later writers have, with their usual elaborateness,

---

hearth which every Brahman is enjoined to keep and pay homage to). When rubbing ashes he generally recites the prayer to Siva taken from the Taittiriya Aranyaka (सद्योजातम् प्रपद्यामि &c.,). The three horizontal lines may be supposed to typify the three functions of Siva—creating, preserving and destroying. The worshippers of Vishnu use Gôpî Chandana, a kind of white earth from Dvârakâ. The upright mark denotes the impress of the God Vishnu's feet, and the red line mark in the centre has been supposed to typify Lakshmi.

* Some say that *másha* is the central line on the palm and quote a verse to that effect. हस्तमध्यगतारेखा माष इत्यभिधीयते.

encumbered it with numerous details to the extent of making it a tedious ceremony. To such as are curious, the following details, which for fear of tiring the patience of the reader we have greatly abridged, may perhaps be interesting.

Achamana is said to be of three kinds—*Sruti*, *Smriti*, and *Purána*. Directions for Srutyâchamana are given in the Taittiriya Aranyaka where it is said that the following mantra :—

विद्युदसि विद्यमे पाप्मानं ऋतात्सत्यमुपैमि ।

'Thou art lightning. Remove my sins. Through Truth I attain unto Truth,' should be recited, and the hands should be washed, water sipped three times, the palm washed again, and the head, the eyes, the ears, and the sides of the nose should be touched. Smrityâchamana is sub-divided into two kinds, Srauta and Smârta. Srautâchamana is thus performed; water is sipped thrice, accompanied by the recitation of the three padas of Gâyatri in succession. Then twenty one parts of the body are touched while the following twenty-one mantras are recited—the nine ablingas—आपोहिष्ठा &c. &c, the seven Vyahritis *i.e.*, the names of the seven worlds preceded by the sacred syllable Om, the three pâdâs of Gâyatrî-siras (*i.e.*) ओमापोज्योतीरसोमृतं &c.

Smârtâchamana is laid down by Manu, Yâjnavalkya and other Smriti writers. Water is sipped thrice, the lips are washed and the mouth and the several sensory organs are touched. Some of the details are differently given by others. Purânâchamana also is variously given by different writers. Water is sipped thrice, and several parts of the body are touched, each single operation being accompanied by the repetition of a distinct name of Vishnu or Siva.

After the Achamana the Smartas usually recite a benedictory prayer to *Vighnesvara*. शुक्लांबरधरं विष्णुं शशिवर्णं चतुर्भुजं ।

प्रसन्नवदनं ध्यायेत् सर्वविघ्नोपशान्तये ॥ *Sukla—ambara—dharam*=wearing a white garment, *Vishnum*=pervading all space, *Sas'ivarnam*=having the colour of the moon, *Chatur-bhujam*=having four hands, *Prasannavada-nam*=elephant-faced, *Dhyâyêt*=one should pray to, *Sarva—vighna—upas'antayê*—for the assuagement of all obstacles.

Then comes *Prânâyâma* (the restraining of the vital breath). This process consists of three distinct acts. 1. *Pûraka i.e.* pressing in the right nostril with the fingers and drawing in the breath through the left, and then pressing in the left nostril and drawing in the breath through the right. 2. *Kumbhaka i. e.* pressing in both nostrils with the finger and the thumb, or with all the fingers and holding in the breath as long as possible. 3. *Rêchaka i. e.* pressing in the right nostril with the thumb and expelling the breath through the left and then pressing in the left nostril, and expelling the breath through the right. While each process is being gone through, the Gâyatri preceded by the seven Vyâhritis (*i. e.* ओं भूः &c.) and followed by the Siromantra (*i. e.* ओमापो ज्योतीरसो &c.) is mentally recited, and when facility is acquired in the process of retention, the same is mentally recited as long as possible.

The suppression of breath which is the special aim of *Prânâyâma* is a preliminary Yôga practice and aids us in fixing our mind on the Supreme Being who is meditated upon, in concentrating our thoughts on Him and in placing ourselves in the proper attitude of devotion. Stories are current among us of Yogins who have by such practices been able to abstract their thoughts entirely from their surroundings, with their minds firmly fixed elsewhere.

Then comes the *Sankalpa* or determination. Man is thought to be fickle-minded and likely to be easily drawn away from any undertaking unless he should sit to it with a fixed resolve. The two hands, are brought together, with the right palm over the left and placed on the right thigh. This attitude is indicative of vow-taking among us. The Sankalpa mantra is मम उपात्त समस्तदुरितक्षयद्वार परमेश्वरप्रीत्यर्थं प्रातः (*or* सायं) सन्ध्यामुपाशिष्ये.

Meaning. *Mama*=my, *Upâtta—samasta-durita—kshaya—dvâra*=through the removal of all sins that have adhered to me—*Parames'vara—prîti—artham*=for the purpose of acquiring the favour of the Supreme Lord—*Prâtah* or *Sâyam Sandhyâm*=the morning or the evening Sandhyâ, *Upâs'ishye* =I worship. In the case of *Mâdhyâhnika* we say *Mâdhyâhnikam Karishye*=I perform *Mâdhyâhnikam*.

Then comes *Mârjana* or sprinkling with water—a mode of self-baptism performed by the worshipper sprinkling water on the head while the following verses are recited.

1. आपो हि ष्ठा मयोभुवः । तान ऊर्जे दधातन ।
महे रणाय चक्षसे ॥

2. यो वः शिवतमो रसः । तस्य भाजयतेह नः ।
उशतीरिव मातरः ॥

3. तस्मा अरं गमाम वः । यस्य क्षयाय जिन्वथ ।
आपो जनयथा च नः ॥

They are the first three verses of the 9th Sûkta of the 10th Mandala in the Rig Veda. They occur also in the Taittirîya Samhitâ (4th Kânda 1st Pras'na 5th Anuvâka.) They are also found in the 1st Mandala of the Atharva Veda with slight modifications and in several places in the Taittirîya Aranyaka. The literal meaning is given below.

1. *Apah*=Oh waters! *Hi*=indeed, *Stha* =you are, *Mayobhuvah*=the sources of happiness; *Tâh*=those (you), *Nah*=us, *Urje* =food, *Dadhâtana*=grant, *Chakshase*=for

sight, *Mahe*=great, *Ranâya*=(and) delightful.

Oh waters! you are indeed the sources of all comforts. Being such, grant us food so that our senses may grow strong and give us joy.

2. *Yah*=which (is), *Vah*=your, *Sivatamah*=most blissful, *Rasah*=essence, *Tasya*=of that, *Iha*=here, *Nah*=us, *Bhâjayata*=make the recipients, *Iva*=as, *Us'atîh*=affectionate, *Mâtarah*=*mothers*.

That essence of yours which is the most blissful, make us the recipients thereof, as affectionate mothers (feed their children with milk from their breast).

3. *Yasya Kshayâya*=on account of whose existence, *Jinvatha*=you are pleased, *Tasmai*=that, *Aram*=enough, *Gamâma*=may we have. *Apah*=oh waters! *Nah*=us, *Janayatha*=grant offspring.

May we be obtain enough of that essence of yours, the existence of which within you makes you feel glad. Oh waters! grant us offspring.

This *rik* has thus been interpreted by Haradattâchârya and Nârâyana Yatíndra in their commentary on the *Sandhyâ*. Vidyâranya offers a slightly different interpretation, thus: We come to you, till we be satisfied, for that food by the existence of which within you, you please herbs and plants; and he has also given another interpretation, thus: We quickly invoke you for the destruction of those sins which you please us by destroying.

Comment. 1. Haradattâchârya quotes a *sloka* in this connection.

आपो हिष्ठाः सुप्रसिद्धाः
नवपादा भवन्ति ते ।
पादे पादे क्षिपेद्वारि
ब्रह्महत्या व्यपोहति ॥

'These *Mantras*—Apohishthâ &c., are well-known. They have nine feet. Water is to be sprinkled (on the head) while each foot is being recited. It will wash away even the sin of Brahmicide.'

2. Nârâyana Yatîndra prefaces his interpretation of these riks with these remarks: आपोहिष्ठादिमन्त्राणां श्रीपाञ्चरात्रादि सच्छास्त्रेषु परमात्मादेवतेत्यभिधानात् अत्रत्याः देवताशब्दाः परमात्मनारायणवाचकाः । अतः अन्यपरतया प्रतीयमानानामपि शब्दानां नामरूपव्याकरणश्रुत्या परमात्मपरत्वं हि वेदान्ते निर्णीतम् ॥

'These *Mantras* are regarded in sacred works like the Pâncharâtras as addressed to the Supreme Lord. We should therefore regard the address here as directed to the Lord (and not to the waters). The Vedânta has established in the Vedic passage relating to the analysis of names and forms (Chhand. Upanis VI) that even words which *appear* to denote other things signify really the Supreme Being.' The Vedic bards were genuine lovers of nature. They had '*the divine afflatus*,' in them. This 'divine afflatus', like gunpowder stored up, required a spark to liberate it and set it at work. Nature in her different manifestations furnished the required spark, and the mind of the Vedic seer 'pregnant with celestial fire,' poured itself out 'in profuse strains of unpremeditated art'. The rapturous song was *really* directed to the Supreme Being; but the more immediate inspirer of the song, the particular aspect of nature which appealed to his feelings had the honor of the *form*.

From the Rig Veda, Prof. Max Müller says "we learn a lesson, which it is well to learn, and which we can hardly learn anywhere else.........how the Beyond or the Infinite was named by different names in order to bring it near the mind of man, to make it for a time comprehensible, until, when name after name had proved of no avail, a nameless God was left to answer best the restless cravings of the human heart." ('India—What can it teach us?'—Lect. V.)

3. Water is here regarded as the source of life, as things that sustain life cannot grow in the absence of rain. The Vedic seer prays in these *riks* for this life-sustaining essence whereby his senses may grow strong, his intellect clear, and he himself, strong enough to bear children (propagation of the line being considered a religious duty which one owes to one's fathers).

4. *Janayatha*. This word is taken by Vidyâranya and Haradattâchârya to mean 'make us have children'; but Nârâyana Yatîndra interprets it to mean 'bring us into existence.' He quotes from the Upanishads to show that what we usually call birth is not birth in the highest sense of the term; there is a higher and nobler birth—the springing of divine knowledge. "विद्या तत् संजनयति तत् श्रेष्ठं जन्म." This divine knowledge—the realisation of the Supreme Soul—is, he says, what has been called

'*S'ivatamah Rasah*' or 'the most blissful essence' in these riks. This bliss alone is *eternal*; all other joys, the most lasting of them, are but transient. As the saying goes, आविरिञ्चादमंगलम्, all conditions of existence up to the exalted position of Brahma the creator—are but miserable.

But what is meant by saying that waters possess this most blissful essence—divine wisdom? Nârâyana Yatîndra thus answers the question. Mere water cannot bestow earthly or heavenly happiness. The Ganges, Setu and other sacred places bestow great happiness only through their special relation to God. We have a passage in the Kaushi. Upanishad where the waters are said to contend for supremacy with others. Waters, in this passage, are taken to refer to the Deity presiding over the waters. Similarly the term *waters* here means the Supreme Lord. And what is the most blissful essence that the Lord can grant us? It is spiritual insight. The springing of this spiritual vision which leads to the realisation of the Universal Self is the second and far more important birth and it is this second birth that is prayed for in the riks.

Thus far Nârâyana Yatindra. Western scholars who see in the hymns of the Rig Veda the primitive simplicity of a race that have just awakened to the wonders of nature around them would consider all this as ingenuity wasted in the attempt to read later philosophy into the primitive hymns. Perhaps they might be right. But the orthodox view is that Truth is *one*, and *eternal*; it may appear in several garbs --one way in the Samhitas, another way in the Upanishads and a third way in the Purânas; but the truth underneath all these disguises is the same.

5. The three verses recited are in Gâyatrì metre. A verse in Gâyatrí metre has three pâdas (feet), each foot having eight

syllables. Water is sprinkled over the head and other parts of the body, each time a foot is recited. Then comes the *mantra* for tasting water for self-purification. There are three *mantras*—one for the morning service, the same with slight modifications, as required for the evening service, and a third for the mid-day service. These *mantras* form respectively the 25th, the 24th and the 23rd Aunvâkas of the 10th Prapâthaka of the Taittirîya Aranyaka. The morning *mantra* is this :—

सूर्यश्चमामन्युश्चमन्युपतयश्चमन्युकृतेभ्यः । पापेभ्यो रक्षन्ताम् । यद्रात्र्या पापमकार्षम् । मनसावाचाहस्ताभ्याम् । पद्भ्यामुदरेणशिश्ना । रात्रिस्तदवलुंपतु । यत्किञ्चदुरितंमयि । इदमहंमाममृतयोनौ । सूर्येज्योतिषिजुहोमिस्वाहा ॥

For the evening service अग्निश्च is substituted for सूर्यश्च, अह्ना for रात्र्या, अहस् for रात्रिः and सत्ये for सूर्ये.

Sûryascha = the sun and, *Mâ* = me, *Man-*

yuscha = *Krodhâbhimânî Devah* = the Lord presiding over anger, *Manyupatayah* = *Krôdhasvâminah* = *Tanniyâmakâh* = the Gods that help a man to restrain his anger, *Manyukritebhyah Pâpebhyah* = from the sins caused by (my) anger, *Rakshantâm* = may (these Gods) protect (me by destroying those sins). *Râtryâ* = *Râtrau* = in the night, *Yad Pâpam* = what sin, *Akârsham* = I committed, *Manasâ—vâchâ—hastâbhyâm—padbhyâm—udarena—s'is'nâ*=by mind, speech, hands, feet, belly (i. e. appetite), and the sensual organ, *Tatsarvam* = all that, *Râtrih Avalumpatu* = may the (Lord presiding over the departed) night remove. *Yat—kim—cha—duritam* = whatever other sin (there is), *Mayi* = in me, *Idam* = all this (sin), *Mâm* = (and) myself, *Aham* = I, *Amritayonau—Sûrye—jyotishi* = in the self-luminous light i.e. the sun, the immortal First Cause, *Juhomi*=I sacrifice, *Svâhâ*=(and for that purpose), may this (purified water) be well offered (as libation in the sacrificial fire i.e. my mouth).

In the evening service, where *Satye* is substituted for *Sûrye*, *Satye* is taken by Sâyana to mean *Bâdharahite*=free from affliction.

The whole *mantra* means, 'May Súrya (or Agni, in the evening), and the God of anger, and the lords presiding over anger, save me from the sins caused by anger. Whatever sin I have committed, by mind (i.e. sinful thoughts), speech (i.e. by speaking sinful words—lies &c.), hands, feet (i.e. by doing sinful deeds), belly (i.e. by eating impure things) and the sensual organ, may the Lord of the departed night (or day) remove all that. Whatever other sin there may be in me,* and myself, I

* We have followed Sâyana's interpretation. Nârâyana Yatindra takes 'whatever other sin (there may be) in me' with '*avalumpatu*,' thus—'remove all that and whatever other sin there may be in me.'

sacrifice in the self-luminous light, the eternal First Cause (Sûrya or Satya). (As an emblem of such a sacrifice, I pour down this consecrated water as libation in my mouth which shall be the sacrificial fire). May this be well offered!'

1. One or two remarks in this connection may not be amiss. Yâska says in the Nirukta, "The Vedic Gods are resolvable into three—Agni whose place is on the earth, Indra or Vâyu whose place is in the atmosphere and Sûrya whose place is in the sky. These again are resolvable into one—the Supreme Being."

2. It is said in the Vedas that the energy of the sun passes on to Agni in the evening, "सौरंतेजस्सायमग्निं संक्रमते": also compare, "दिनान्ते निहितंतेजः सवित्रेव हुताशनः" (Raghuvamsa IV). Hence the substitution of Agni for Sûrya in the evening.

3. But as we have elsewhere pointed

out, whether it be Súrya or Agni, Manyu or Varuna, that is addressed, he is addressed as a symbol of the Supreme, as the 'manifestation of Him who is infinitely beyond human ken.'

4. This prayer recognises that anger is the chief source of sins and begs for control over this 'Tartar chief of passions.'

5. *Myself with all my sins I sacrifice in the Eternal Light.* Consciousness of sin and unconditional sacrifice of oneself at the footstool of Divine mercy are recognised as the only means of deliverance from sin. The closing words of the prayer seem to say—and in such sweet, simple language—"Oh Lord, such as I am, take me with all my sins and dispose of me as thou wilt." The efficacy of such a prayer is not in any extraneous granting of the boon required as is generally supposed, but in the heartfelt words inducing a state of mind in harmony with the sentiment expressed; this

state conduces to a loftier frame, a lifting up of the soul, which is the first step towards the realisation of the *summum bonum* of life—the emancipation of the soul from all earthly trammels.

6. This unconditional sacrifice is symbolically represented by pouring a small quantity of water into one's mouth. The water represents the sinner with his sins and the pouring down typifies the act of sacrificing. During the Vedic period sacrifice was a *reality* to the sacrificer. His fervid faith could *realise* the picture which his imagination painted in such glowing colours before his mental vision. This reality passed away in later times, "when Sphageology was only an idea—a warm, inspiring and vivid idea. It had ceased to be an image.........Gradually the idea passed into a symbol and the symbol was petrified into a form."*

* M. M. Kunte's 'Vicissitudes of Aryan civilization in India'—p. 144.

7. *Manyupatayah* = Haradatta and Nârâyana Yatindra take it to mean 'desire, hatred, lust &c." 'May these protect me' is taken to mean 'may I, through the grace of God, be kept from their evil influence.'

8. The Yajurvedins and the Rigvedins use these *mantras* for the morning and the evening purificatory libation. The Sâmavedins use an abbreviated form, thus: In the morning, they taste a small quantity of water with the following *mantra*. अहश्च मा आदित्यश्च पुनातुस्वाहा, "May (the presiding Deity of) the day and the sun make me pure! May this water be well offered!" The evening *mantra* is रात्रिश्च मा वरुणश्च पुनातुस्वाहा, "May (the presiding Deity of) the night and Varuna make me pure! May this water be well offered!" As will be explained in the sequel, the sun typifies the Supreme Lord as presiding over the day and Varuna represents the Lord as presiding over the night.

The mantra for the mid-day service is this:

आपः पुनन्तु पृथिवीं पृथिवी पूता पुनातु मां। पुनन्तु ब्रह्मणस्पतिः ब्रह्मपूता पुनातु मां। यदुच्छिष्टमभोज्यं यद्वा दुश्चरितं मम। सर्वं पुनन्तु मामापोऽसतां च प्रतिग्रहं स्वाहा।

Meaning. *Apah Punantu*=may the waters purify, *Prithivim*=the earth (by pouring down rain), *Prithivi—pûtâ—punâtu*=may the purified earth purify, *Mâm*=me, *Punantu* =may (the waters) purify, *Brahmanaspatih* =*Vedasya Patim**=*Vedasya Pratipâlakam*

---

* We have, here as elsewhere, followed the interpretation of Sâyana. He takes *patih* (nom.) as equivalent to *patim* (acc.). This apparently forced interpretation seems to be justified by the following considerations: 1. If *Patih* be taken in the nominative, the next sentence *Brahma Pûtâ Punâtu Mâm* would be a needless repetition of the same meaning. 2. *Patih* in the nom. sing. will have to be taken with *punantu*, a predicate in the plural—a grammatical difficulty equally perplexing. Viewed in any light, the passage is a grammatical puzzle and defies the rules of concord. Others make out the passage thus:

Achâryam = the Achârya who preserves the (teaching of the) Veda, *Brahma* = the Veda, *Pûtâ* = *Swayampûtam* *Sat* = holy (by itself) *Punâtu* = may (it) purify, *Mâm* = me, *Yat—uchhishtam* = what leavings of food (I may have eaten), *Abhojyam* = what things unfit to eat (I may have eaten), *Yadvâ—duscharitam—mama* = or any other improper act of mine, *Asatâm—pratigraham—cha* = and the receipt of gifts from the unworthy, *Sarvam* = all (that) sin, (understand *parihritya* = destroying), *Mâm* = me, *Punantu* = may (the waters) purify: *Svâhâ* (And for this purpose &c.)

The *mantra* means this—(i) May the waters purify the earth by pouring down rain. May the earth thus purified make me pure. (ii) May the waters purify my

---

Brahmanaspatih = may the Lord of the Veda, *punâtu* = purify (me). *Brahmapûtâ* (*Prithivî*) = the earth purified by the Veda, *Punâtu* *Mâm* = purify me. This interpretation is open to the objection of needless repetition.

spiritual preceptor and may the Veda (as taught by the purified preceptor) purify me. (iii) Whatever leavings of another's food and whatever impure things I may have eaten, whatever I may have received as gift from the unworthy, may the waters destroy all that sin and purify me; and for this purpose, I pour this sanctified water as libation down my mouth.

This *mantra* contains three distinct prayers.

1. May timely rains fertilise the earth and make people prosperous and happy and may my heart be purified from all taint of selfishness by rejoicing in the prosperity of all living beings. What a beautiful prayer! To wish for a heart that rejoices in the well-being of all things on earth—not a heart 'concentred all in self'! With what divine intuition is the point grasped, that the heart of man is purified only by forgetting self and identifying its joys with those

of "all living beings", that unselfish love for all things on earth is the only 'stream of tendency which makes for righteousness.' This is the burden of the Brahman's song. "लोकाः समस्ताः सुखिनो भवन्तु." "May all the world be happy!" Every public ceremony that the Brahman engages in invariably ends with this prayer. When we hear this noble refrain from the lips of Brahmans—and times without number have we heard it—we cannot help thinking that a people with such noble sentiments ever on their lips cannot but be god-favoured.

2. The second prayer is directed nearer home. May my spiritual preceptor be happy—my Achârya who by laying before me the treasures of Vedic wisdom has enraptured my soul and made it 'live, and move and have its being' in the Universal Paramâtman,—and may the wisdom of the divine Veda soak my soul through and through, and make my heart a fit abode

for the 'Nameless One.' Comment is superfluous.

3. May the waters absolve me of the sins of having eaten impure things and having accepted gifts from the wicked. Indulgence in 'forbidden food' rouses up the carnal instincts of man, and obligation to the wicked implies the commission of wicked deeds to secure their favour and involves an iniquitous indebtedness, perhaps to be iniquitously discharged. The object of their special mention is to put oneself on guard against these temptations, to prevent their recurrence if they cannot be altogether avoided.

Comment.—Haradatta offers a different interpretation of the opening portion: May this consecrated water (which I am about to use as libation) purify my body which is of earthy essence. May this purified earthy essence—my body—purify me, the spirit dwelling within.

Nârâyana Yatîndra takes '*Brahmanaspatih*' to mean "the Supreme Lord revealed by the Scriptures."

This *mantra* is used by the followers of all the three Vedas.

After tasting water with the *mantra* for self-purification, a second self-baptism is performed, this time beginning with the *mantra*, *Dadhikrâvno &c.* and followed by the *Ablingas*, *Apohishtha &c.* As we have already given the meaning of *Ablinga mantras* with the remarks suggested thereby, we shall here give the meaning of the first alone.

This *mantra* occurs in the Rig Veda IV *Mandala*, 39th *Sûkta*. It also occurs in the 11th *Anuvâka* of the 5th *Prapâthaka* of the 1st *Kanda* of the *Taittirîya Samhita*. It runs thus.

दधि॒क्राव्णो॑ अकारिषं जि॒ष्णोरश्व॑स्य वा॒जिनः॑ ।

सु॒र॒भि नो॒ मुखा॑ कर॒त्प्रण॒ आयूं॑षि तारिषत् ॥

Dadhikrâvnah = of the God Dadhikrâvan, *Jishnoh*=victorious, *As'vasya*=*Vyâpakasya* = pervading (all), *Vâjinah*=*Vegavatah*=of great speed (understand *Stutim*=praise), *Akârisham* = I make ; *Nah* = our, *Mukhâ* = *Mukhâni* = mouths *i.e.* the eyes and the other senses, *Surabhi* = *Surabhîni* = fragrant, *Karat* = *Karotu* = may he make, *Nah* = our, *Ayûmshi* = life, *Pratârishat* = may he lengthen.

I sing the praise of the God Dadhikrâvan, who is victorious, all-prevading and who moves with great speed. May he make our mouths (and the senses) fragrant and may he prolong our lives!

1. *Dadhikrâvan*—This God is often mentioned in the Veda and is the subject of Sûktas 38, 39 and 40 of the fourth *Mandala* of the Rig Veda and the 44th Sûkta of the 7th *Mandala* of the same. He seems to be described in these places as a kind of divine horse. Sometimes he is considered as a creation of heaven and

earth, sometimes of Mitra and Varuna, and is invoked in the morning with Agni, Ushas and the As'vins. Sir Monier Williams would derive the word from *dadhi* = curd (which he takes to represent dew) and *kri* = to scatter, in allusion to the rising sun spreading dew and hoarfrost like milk.

Sâyana regards *Dadhikrâvan* as a form of Agni. He says in his commentary on the Rig Veda, (*Mandala* 4, Sûkta 39, *rik* 2): अश्वरूपं वा देवं। अग्नेरश्वरूपस्यैव दधिकारव्यत्वात्। अग्नेः तद्रूपत्वं ब्राह्मणे समाम्नातं। तानग्निः अश्वो भूत्वाभ्यद्रवदिति।

"Agni in the form of a horse is called *Dadhikra*; the equine form of Agni has been declared in the Brâhmana thus: Agni, becoming a horse, pursued them."

Haradatta says: 'दधि = हवींषि, क्रामति = प्राप्नोति इति दधिक्रावा कश्चिद्देवविशेषः, अग्निरित्यन्ये. 'A certain deity who receives the oblations or Agni as others have it.' Nârayâna Yatindra takes the term to denote 'Him who pervades the Universe—the Supreme Being.'

2. Whether it be Agni or Sûrya (and both are regarded only as different forms of the same Divine Energy) that is represented in this hymn as *Jishnoh*, victorious in his fight with the powers of darkness, as *As'vasya*, illuminating the universe with his bright rays, and as *Vâjinah*, moving with great speed in his triumphal procession, he is an apt emblem of heaven's perpetual King who dispels our ignorance, illumines our heart with divine wisdom and flies to our succour on the wings of grace.

3. The object of this second performance of *Márjana* is set forth in the prayer embodied in the second half of the hymn, where the worshipper asks for the gift of sweet speech (lit—fragrant mouth) wherewith to approach His throne with heart-felt *Hâllelujahs*, and long life to be devoted to His service and adoration.

The Yajur Vedins and the Sâmavedins

use this *rik* for the second *Mârjana;* but the Ṛigvedins recite the whole of the Sûkta which begins with *Apohishtha.* The remaining *riks* and their translation are given below.

शंनो॑ दे॒वीर॒भिष्ट॑य॒ आपो॑ भवन्तु पी॒तये॑ ।
शंयोर॒भिस्र॑वन्तु नः ॥ १ ॥

'May the divine waters conduce to our happiness, to our sacrifice and our drink; may they ward off diseases and cure those that we have; may they be sprinkled over us.

ईशा॑ना॒ वार्या॑णां॒ क्षय॑न्तीश्चर्षणी॒नां ।
अ॒पो या॑चामि भेष॒जं ॥ २ ॥

Waters, who are the controllers of the cereals and the sustainers of men, I pray to you for happiness (through the removal of my sins.)

अ॒प्सु मे॒ सोमो॑ अब्रवीद॒न्तर्विश्वा॑नि भेषजा ।
अ॒ग्निं च॑ वि॒श्वशं॑भुवं ॥ ३ ॥

Soma has told me that in the midst of the waters are all medicaments and Agni who gives happiness to all the world.

आपःपृणीत भेषजं वरूथं तन्वे३ मम ।
ज्योक् च सूर्यं दृशे ॥ ४ ॥

Oh waters! Grant, for my body, a full supply of medicament that can cure all diseases; so that I may see the sun for a long time.

इदमापःप्रवहत यत्किं च दुरितं मयि ।
यद्वाहमभिदुद्रोह यद्वा शेप उतानृतम् ॥ ५ ॥

Whatever sin there is in me, whatever I have done in treachery, what sin I have contracted by cursing or by uttering untruth, may the waters remove all this!

आपो अद्यान्वचारिषं रसेन समगस्महि ।
पयस्वानग्न आगहि तं मा संसृज वर्चसा ॥ ६ ॥

This day have I entered the waters and united with their essence; Oh, Agni, residing in the waters, do thou come and unite me (who have bathed) with lustre.

After this second sprinkling, the Rig-vedins recite a prayer for the forgiveness of sins. This prayer is called *Aghamarshana* (*i.e.* a prayer for the forgiveness of sins). It is the last but one *Sûkta* of the Rigveda. A little water is taken up in *anjali* (both the hands being brought together and hollowed), air is drawn in through the left nostril, and, after suppression of breath for a while, is expelled through the right nostril. The Sûkta is recited during this *Prânâyâma* and after the recital, the water is thrown down to the left of the worshipper. The *Aghamarshana* hymn with the translation is given below: (The seer of the hymn is also called by the same name).

ऋतं च सत्यं चाभीद्धात्तपसोऽध्यजायत।
ततोरात्र्यजायत ततःसमुद्रो अर्णवः ॥ १ ॥

From the *tapas* performed (the contemplation made by Brahman, previous to creation or, according to another interpretation of Sâyana, from the self-luminous *Paramâtman*) sprang Truth in mind and Truth in word; then was born Night (and Day); then the Ocean.

समुद्रादर्णवादधि संवत्सरो अजायत ।
अहोरात्राणि विदधद्विश्वस्य मिषतोवशी ॥ २ ॥

After the Ocean was born the Year (*i. e.* the several divisions of time); having created (all beings represented by) day and night, He is the Lord of all that winks.

सूर्या चंद्रमसौ धाता यथापूर्वमकल्पयत् ।
दिवं च पृथिवीं चांतरिक्षमथो स्वः ॥ ३ ॥

The sun and the moon, the blissful heaven, the earth and the sky—(all these)—the Creator brought into existence as in the former ages.*

---

* (For a detailed explanation of these *riks*, the reader is referred to the commentary on the *Purushasûkta* by the author).

All the ceremonial up to this point should have been gone through before the actual appearance of the sun above the horizon. The worshipper has by these acts of purification, both internal and external, made himself worthy to salute the Lord who resides in the orb of the rising luminary and render Him homage in true Brahman style, by what is called the *Arghya*. The *Arghya* is a respectful offering of water (sometimes mixed with flowers and some other ingredients) to any respectable guest. This form of salutation has been in use among us from time immemorial. In the *Sandhyâ*, it is an act of homage to the Lord in the sun. The worshipper offers water and throws it in the air, either from a boat-shaped copper vessel or from the two open hands hollowed and joined together, with the sacred thread put round the two thumbs. He thus throws water upwards towards the sun three times, each time reciting the Gâyatrî prayer.

The Gâyatrî prayer runs thus.

ओं । तत्सवितुर्वरेण्यं भर्गो देवस्य धीमहि ।

धियो योनः प्रचोदयात् ॥ R. V. III—62—10.

This prayer is called *Gâyatrî* from the metre of the same name. For though there are other hymns in the same metre this is the *Gâyatrî* hymn *par excellence* and is believed to contain the sum and substance of all Vedic teaching.

Sâyana proposes three interpretations. The first is this. *Tat Savitur Devásya*=of that Lord, the Creator of the Universe, *Varenyam*=adorable, *Bhargah*=light, *Dhîmahi*=we meditate on. *Yah**=who, *Nah* =our, *Dhiyah*=actions or intellectual faculties, *Prachodayât*=may stimulate (so that we may grasp the eternal Truth.)

---

* Sâyana thinks that *yah* may also be taken to be equivalent to the neuter *yat* and the adjective clause taken with *bhargas*, in which case *tat* should be also referred to *bhargas*, thus meaning, 'that light &c.'

We meditate on the adorable light of the Supreme Creator of the Universe. May He (or it, the light) (existing in our minds) guide our intellects (in the pursuit of Truth).

Sâyana makes the next interpretation applicable to Súrya thus: *Yah* = who (*i.e.* which sun), *Nah* = our, *Dhiyah* = *Karmâni* = duties, *Prachodayât* = *Prerayati* = directs, *Savitur* = of the sun, *Tat* = *Sarvaih Dris'yamânatayâ Prasidham* = well-known as being seen by all, *Varenyam* = (and hence) adorable, *Bhargas* = *Tejomandalam* = *the halo of light*, *Dhîmahi* = we think of.

We think of the well-known adorable halo of light of the sun, who (rousing us from sleep) directs us to our (several) duties. Sâyana bases his third interpretation on the Gopatha Brâhmana of the Atharva Veda, where *bhargas* is taken to mean food. "We obtain food through the favour of that sun who guides our intellects."

But it is clear that Sâyana prefers the first meaning. The second interpretation does not materially differ from the first. For it is everywhere recognised in the Vedas that there is no distinction between the Supreme Lord who resides as light in the sun and Him who lives in our heart, stimulating our understanding and guiding us aright.

The prayer speaks for itself. It says, "Oh Lord! I think of Thy glory. Illumine my heart with Thy divine grace and guide me aright." We can think of no better words with which to approach the Supreme Lord.

Some additional remarks on the *Gâyatri* will be found in the comment on the *Prâ-nâyâma* mantrá (later on).

If this *Arghyapradâna* be not made in the proper time an additional offering of *Arghya* is made to expiate this sin.

The Yajurvedins offer three *Arghyas* in

the morning and the evening, and two *Arghyas* in the noon and one additional expiatory *Arghya* on each occasion. All the *Arghyas* are offered with the *Gâyatrî mantra.* The Sâmavedins do the same; but the expiatory *Arghya* is not offered with the *Gâyatrî* but with three different *riks*, for the morning, the noon and the evening. The Rigvedins also use the same *riks* for the expiatory *Arghyas* and offer the three morning and evening ordinary *Arghyas* with the Gâyatrî; at noon, they offer the first *Arghya* with the *rik* आकृष्णेन &c., the second with the *mantra* हंस: &c., and a third with the *Gâyatrî*.

The morning expiatory *Arghya mantra* is,

यद॒द्य कच्च॑ वृत्रहन्नु॒दगा॑ अ॒भिसू॑र्य ।
सर्वं॒ तदि॑न्द्र ते॒ वशे॑ ॥ R. V. viii—93—4.

Oh thou Súrya, (who art the same as) Indra, slayer of the Asura Vritra (the demon of drought), whatever thy rays shine on this day, all that is under thy control. (It is the sun that rouses all beings into activity and directs them in their several pursuits).

The mid-day expiatory *Arghya mantra* is:

प्रातर्देवीमदितिं जोहवीमि
मध्यंदिन उदिता सूर्यस्य ।
राये मित्रावरुणा सर्वतातेळे
तोकाय तनयाय शंयोः ॥ R. V. v.—69—3.

I invoke the Goddess Aditi in the morning (and) at noon when the sun has risen up; Oh Mitra and Varuna, I praise you in the sacrifice for wealth, for children, for children's children, for the assuagement of all evils and for prosperity.

The Sâmavedins use the following *rik* for the mid-day expiatory *Arghya*.

उद्घेदभि श्रुतामघं वृषभं नर्यापसं ।
अस्तारमेषिसूर्य ॥ R. V. viii—93—1.

Oh Sûrya, thou risest for (receiving the

oblations of) the benefactor of men, famed for his wealth, who showers wealth (on the poor) and who is liberal.

The evening expiatory *Arghya mantra* is :

नतस्य मायया चनरिपुरीशीतमर्त्यः ।
यो अग्नये ददाश हव्यदातिभिः । R. V. viii-23-15.

He who, with officiating priests at a sacrifice, offers oblations to Agni, over him not even an enemy with *mâyic* (magical) powers has power.

The Rigvedic *mantra* for the first mid-day *Arghya* is :

आकृष्णेन रजसा वर्तमानो निवेशयन्नमृतं मर्त्यंच ।
हिरण्ययेन सविता रथेनादेवोयाति भुवनानि पश्यन् ॥

R. V. i—35—2.

The Lord *Savitri* every day appears in the blue heavens, sustaining gods and men ; he comes in a golden chariot, beholding all the worlds.

The Rigvedic *mantra* for the second mid-day *Arghya* is :

हंसः शुचिषद्वसुरन्तरिक्षसद्धोता वेदिषदतिथिर्दुरोणसत् ।
नृषद्वरसदृतसद्व्योमसदब्जा गोजा ऋतजा
अद्रिजा ऋतम् ॥ R. V. iv—40—5.

This *mantra* occurs also in the Taitt. Aran. (X–10) and is there a little differently interpreted by Sâyana, the same commentator.

The ever-travelling sun in the solar orb, the air in the mid-heavens, the adorable *Gârhapatya* fire at the altar, the fire in the household hearth, the vital spark in man, the divine essence in sacred places, that which exists in Truth, that which shines in the heavens (*i.e.* the light in the stars), that which has sprung from the waters, that which has sprung from the rays, that which has sprung from Truth, that which rises from the mountain,—all this is the eternal Truth, the universal Paramâtman.

Some Rigvedins offer the first mid-day *Arghya* with this rik and the second and the third with the Gâyatrî.

The worshipper then throws water around himself in the form of a circular ring, with a view to keep off all evil influence from him.

The worshipper then looks at the sun, and touches his heart with his fingers reciting the *mantra*,

असावादित्यो ब्रह्म ।

Asau—this, *Adityah*—Sun, *Brahma* (is) Brahman, the Supreme Lord.

The Lord whom I invoke as residing in the sun is not the visible luminary but the same Supreme Being who lives in my heart and guides me.

The object of this *mantra* seems to be to expressly put the worshipper on guard against supposing that his worship is directed to the physical sun he sees. The Taittirîya Upanishad says: (Taitt. Aran. viii-8) सयश्चायं पुरुषे । यश्चासावादित्ये । स एकः He who exists in man as the *Jivâtman* and He who is visible in the solar orb, He is one. Then the Upanishad goes on to say that he who knows this is emancipated at death from *all* material bonds.

In this connection, a legend as related in the Gopatha Brâhmana of the Atharva Veda is worthy of note. Glâva of the race of Mitra (Maitreya) presumptuously called the learned sage Maudgalya ill-instructed. Maudgalya then called upon Glâva to explain the Sâvitrî. Glâva could not answer the question. Thus humbled, he came to the sage with fuel in hand. That was how those wishing to learn approached their teachers in those days. He said to Maudgalya: "Sir, I beg your pardon. Please enlighten me on the following points. To whom do wise men allude by the phrase सवितुर्वरेण्यम् &c., 'the adorable glory of the God Savitri' and advise me as to what they mean by *Dhiyah* and tell me the courses through which the sun moves on (*prachodayât*)."

Maudgalya replied: 'By *Varênyam*, the wise mean the Vedas and the Chhandas, by *Bhargo Devasya*, aliment (*anna*) and *Dhiyah*, by which the sun moves on (or *prachodayât*) are duties.' Learning this, Glâva requested him saying 'Tell me, who is Savitri and what Sâvitrí'.

Then Maudgalya offers a lengthy explanation and identifies Savitri and Sâvitrí with the following twelve couples: (1) Mind and speech (2) Fire and Earth (3) Vâyu and Ether (4) the Sun and the Sky (5) the Moon and the Stars (6) Day and Night (7) Heat and Cold (8) the cloud and the rain (9) the lightning and thunder (10) life and food (11) the Vedas and Chhandas (12) Sacrifice (*Yajna*) and fee (*Dakshinâ*).

Maudgalya thus concludes his explanation—'Sacrifice is established on the Vedas; the Vedas are established on speech;

speech is established on the mind; the mind on life; life on food; food on earth; the earth on water; water on light; light on Vâyu; Vâyu on Ether; the Ether on Brahmán; Brahman on Brâhmanas acquainted with Brahman. Verily he is conscient of Brahman who knows this. He achieves meritorious acts and sweet odours—he destroys all sins, and enjoys endless grace,—who knows this, as also he who knowing this adores the Upanishad which has the Sâvitrí for its subject'

Dr. Rajendra Lal Mitra L.L.D., in noticing this legend in his edition of the Gopatha Brahmana, offers the following remarks:—This interpretation "is on all fours with the belief of the Hindus that the object adored is Brahman or the Universal Soul, and therefore also of the sun, and not the sun itself as represented by its rays. As the interpretation is the oldest we possess and was given within a short time after the Gâyatrî had been composed, this fact is worthy of note,—particularly as it is at variance with the version given by some European Orientalists, notably by the late Professor Wilson, which makes the Sun itself to be the object of worship. It is of course impossible to say what the author of the *Gâyatrî* himself had in view, but his Indian commentators, both ancient and modern, are at one in believing that he rose from nature up to nature's God, and adored that sublime Luminary which is visible only to the eye of reason, and not the planet we daily see in its course."

We have adduced sufficient evidence from the Sandhyâ prayer itself to show that the Deity contemplated therein is the Universal Brahman and not the visible sun.

The next thing, as is now the practice, is to make offerings of water to the *Sandhyâ*

Devatâ, to the several planets, to Vishnu and to Yama who are invoked by their several names, each time an offering is made. Thus—*Sandhyâm Tarpayâmi i. e.* I make this offering of water to please the Sandhyâ Devatâ &c.; *Kes'avam Tarpayâmi* = I make this offering to please Kesava &c. &c.

But these are *pauranic* additions and no reference is made to them in the Taittirîya Aranyaka. We are of opinion therefore that these additions are inconsistent with the spirit of the *Sandhyâ Vandanam* which is a prayer directed to the "One alone, without a second"

The first part of the ceremony technically called the *Sandhyâ* now closes. Then begins the second part which is called *Japam*. As usual, the *Japam* is also preceded, by an invocation to Ganes'a, a *Prânâyâma* and *Samkalpa* or resolution. This is apparently needless, but our forefathers seem to have proceeded on the principle that we cannot have too much of a good thing. We have already explained the meaning and the object of the prayer to Ganes'a and the *Samkalpa*. We have also explained the *rationale* of the *Prândâyâma* or the restraining of the breath; we will here give the *Prândâyâma mantra* in entire and explain its meaning.

ओंभूः । ओंभुवः । ओ३ँ सुवः । ओंमहः । ओंजनः । ओंतपः । ओ३ँ सत्यं । ओंतत्सवितुर्वरेण्यं भर्गोदेवस्य धीमहि । धियो योनः प्रचोदयात् । ओमापो ज्योतीरसोऽमृतंब्रह्म भूर्भुवःसुवरों ॥ 27th Anu. 10th Prap. Taitt. Aran.

Bhûh, Bhuvah, Suvah, Mahah, Janah, Tapah, Satyam are called the seven *Vyâhritis* and are the names of the seven worlds which are believed to constitute the Universe. Sâyana remarks that these several names are preceded by the monosyllable *Om* as they denote the universe which is the visible manifestation of the Supreme Soul who is represented by *Om*.

Volumes have been written on the syllable *Om*, which is believed to contain the essence of all the teaching of the Veda and the Vedânta. It is thought to be the most expressive and significant of all the names of the Infinite. It first appears in the Brâhmanas and the Upanishads as a mystic monosyllable (such as Gopatha Brahmana and Chhândogyopanishad) and is there set forth as the object of profound religious meditation and as a mysterious agent endowed with supernatural powers. The highest spiritual efficacy is attributed not only to the whole word but also to the three sounds *A*, *U*, *M* of which it consists. In the Purânas *Om* is the mystic name of the Hindu Triad and represents the union of the three gods, *A* denoting Vishnu, *U* Siva, and *M* Brahma. Three in fact is a sacred number with the Hindus and *Om* has been supposed to represent all the sacred Hindu religious triads. It is usually called *Pranava* and in later times, it has been also called *Omkâra*. All sacred writings begin and end with *Om*. All Vedic recitations begin with *Om* and end with *Om*. All the *Bîja* mantras begin with this sacred exclamation and often end with the same. Bhâskara Râya, the learned commentator on the *Lalitâ Sahasra-Nâmâvali* says that thePranava used at the commencement, and at the end of any *mantra* is, as it were, two pegs driven down at the two ends of the *mantra*, to keep the several letters of the *mantra* intact and preserve their religious efficacy.

It has been derived from the root *av* to protect; but some western scholars (notably Professor Bloomfield) are for deriving it from *âm* and regarding it as originally nothing more than a word of solemn affirmation and respectful assent—something like *amen*. Even the Buddhists have not escaped the influence of this word.

They regard *Omkârâ* (f) as the female personification of Divine Energy. Sir Monier Williams notices that the Buddhists use *Om* at the commencement of their *Vidyâ-shadakshari* or mystical formulary in six syllables (*Om mâni padme hum*).

After the seven Vyâhritis comes the Gâyatrí prayer, also preceded by *Om*.

Nârâyana Yatìndra thus interprets the *Pranava*. *A*, he says, represents the Supreme Lord Nârâyana ; the dative termination being implied, *A* means 'To the Supreme Lord'. *U* means 'alone' (and it may also be taken to denote Lakshmî). *M*, the twenty-fifth consonant, denotes the twenty-fifth principle in man namely the spirit or *Jîvâtman*. Thus *Aum* means 'To the Supreme Lord alone, the *Jîvâtman* (is the complement or *Seshabhûta*)'. The *Pranava* represents the vital faith of the *Vis'ishtâdvaitins*, that the human soul is an entity 'that lives and moves and has its being' in the Supreme Lord alone. This interesting interpretation will illustrate how the most contradictory beliefs can be proved to have a basis on one and the same Vedic text.

The use of the *Pranava* at the beginning and at the end of a *mantra*, symbolises, in Nârâyana's view, the fact that everything springs from the Lord and goes to Him in the end.

Haradatta says that the three letters *A*, *U*, *M*, represent the Puranic Trinity—Brahma, Vishnu and Rudra—and the *Pranava* is the symbol of the Supreme Being, of whose essence these gods are.

Others are of opinion that in addition to the three letters *A*, *U*, *M*, which typify the Trinity, there is a fourth sound—an *ardha-mâtra*, in the *Pranava*—which represents a fourth and higher Being—the Param Brahman.

The *Gâyatri* has been similarly interpreted in various ways; and each interpretation has been supported by its adherents by a host of authoritative texts from the Scriptures. The controversy it has given rise to will form a library by itself and all that can be attempted here is but the briefest sketch of the several methods.

1. Sâyana's meaning has been already given and his first interpretation is that which has been accepted by the generality of *Advaitins.*

2. Nârâyana Yatindra: We meditate on the adorable Light of the Lord *Vâsudeva* who sustains the Universe. May He guide our understanding aright!

The Lord Nârâyana Himself is the Light and so the term 'light of Vâsudeva' is to be taken like 'the head of Râhu', Râhu being nothing but the head.

3 Haradatta bases his interpretation on the *Smriti Bhâskara* and takes *Tadbhargas* to refer to the *Paramâtman* who is to be worshipped as residing in the

midst of the Solar orb.

4. The *S'aivites* take the word *Bhargas* as a noun (in the masculine gender with—*a* termination) in apposition with *yah*; So the prayer is addressed to *S'iva*, as the *Maitrâyana*, the *Talavakara* and other *S'rutis* declare that *Bhargas* denotes S'iva; (as, for instance, in the Maitrâyana Upanishad, we have 'एषरुद्रो भर्गाख्यो ब्रह्मवादिनो वदन्ति')

5. The *Sauras* have *prima facie* a strong case in their favour; they take the *Gâyatrî* prayer as addressed to the Sun himself, who is the source of all life. It is needless to say that this is the interpretation of all western scholars.

6. The S'*âktas* take *Savituh* as referring to the Supreme Being who is the source of all life; and *Varenyam Bhargas*, to His *S'akti*. It is this *Sakti* of the Supreme Lord, to whom the adoration is paid in the *Gâyatrî*.

7. S'aṃkara's interpretation is, of course *Vedântic*. That which enlightens our under-

standing is the *Pratyagâtman* which enlightens *Jnâna*, *Buddhi*, and the *Antahkarana* and which is the All-witness. *Tatsavituh* refers to *Paramâtman*, who is of the same nature as *Pratyagâtman*. *Bhargas* is the *Jnâna* which destroys *Avidyâ*. Thus the prayer means: I, *Pratyagâtman*, who am mere witness of the things seen by *Buddhi &c.* meditate on my nature as identical with the *Brahman*.*

The seven *Vyâhritis* have been thus explained by Haradatta.

Om Bhûh: *Bhûh* means existence and so *Om Bhûh* means that the Supreme Being is the only real existence, all things else existing only phenomenally (*Vyâvahârika*, not *Pâramârthika*).

---

* This interpretation of S'aṃkara has been abridged from S. E. Gopalacharulu's translation. We have not met with the original of S'amkara, which, he says, is to be found in Mr. T. Tatia's edition of Rig-Veda Bhashya.

Om Bhuvah, means that all things, even while they exist, exist only in Him.

Om Suvah, means that He is surrounded by wise sages like *Sanaka*, or that He pervades the entire Universe.

Om Mahah means that it is He alone who is to be adored by all desirous of the final bliss.

Om Janah means that it is He who has brought all this Universe into existence.

Om Tapah means that the Sun who illuminates and warms the whole Universe is but a symbol of Him.

Om Satyam means that He is Truth Eternal.

These meanings Haradatta traces from the etymology of the several words. He also remarks that the *Vyâhritis* may be taken to refer to the seven upper (and by implication, also the seven lower) worlds and the pre-fixing of the *Pranava* means that all these worlds have sprung from the Supreme Being.

Yâjnavalkya's explanation of the *Vyâhritis* as translated by Colebrooke, is given below.

"The prayer is preceded by the names of the seven worlds, as epithets of it, to denote its efficacy; signifying that this light pervades and illumines the seven worlds which, situated one above the other, are the seven mansions of all beings; they are called the seven abodes, self-existent in a former period, renovated in this. These seven mysterious words are celebrated as the names of the seven worlds. The place where all beings, whether fixed or movable, exist, is called Earth (*Bhûh*) which is the first world. That in which beings exist a second time, but without sensation, again to become sensible at the close of the period appointed for the duration of the present universe, is the world of Re-existence (*Bhuvah*). The abode of the Good, where cold, heat and light are perpetually produced is named Heaven (*Suvah*). The intermediate region between the upper and the lower worlds is denominated the middle world (*Mahah*). The heaven where animals destroyed in a general conflagration at the close of the appointed period are born again is thence called the world of Births (*Janah*). That in which Sanaka and the sons of Brahma, justified by austere devotion, reside exempt from all dominion is thence named the mansion of the Blessed (*Tapah*). Truth (*Satyam*) the seventh world and the abode of the Brahman is placed on the summit above other worlds. It is attained by true knowledge, by the regular discharge of duties, and by veracity; once attained, it is never lost. Truth is indeed the seventh world, therefore called the sublime world."*

The *Gâyatrî* † is followed by :—

---

* Colebrooke's 'Miscellaneous Essays' Vol. 1.

† The *Gâyatrî* is held to have a fourth *pâda* (which is revealed only to the initiated). This *pâda* means, 'He who is beyond all phenomenon, He is Bliss Eternal. Om.'

ओं आपो ज्योतीरसोऽमृतं ब्रह्म भूर्भुवः सुवरोम् ॥
which is called the *S'iromantra* of the *Gâyatrî*.

Apah = the waters (of rivers and oceans); *Jyotis* = light (of the Sun &c.), *Rasah* = the several tastes or flavours; *Amritam* = the nectar of the Gods—all this and, *Bhûh Bhuvah, Suvah* = the three worlds—all is *Om*, the Universal Soul. Thus the whole *Prânâyâma* mantra means "All the seven worlds are (the visible manifestation of) *Om*, the all-pervading Brahman. We think of the adorable light (glory) of the Lord who shines in our hearts and guides us; may He guide our intellects aright! Water, light, all things that have savour (such as trees, herbs and plants), the nectar of the Gods, the three worlds—in fact everything that is, is Brahman, the Universal Soul."

This explanation of the *Gâyatrî-Siras* is based on Sâyana's commentary.

Haradatta explains it thus:

Om Apah means 'He pervades all that exists'. *Jyotis* means 'He is Self-luminous Intellectual Light'. *Rasah* means 'He is Bliss'; in other words, the three words indicate that He is *Sat*, *Chit*, and *Ananda*. *Amritam Brahma* means that He (who is characterised by *Sat*, *Chit*, and *Ananda*) is the imperishable Brahman. *Bhûr Bhuvah Suvah* means 'He creates, sustains, and destroys all the worlds.'

While holding the breath through the *Prânâyâmic* process the worshipper should concentrate his mind on the ideas expressed by the above *mantra* and place himself in an attitude of mind consonant with the thoughts running through it.

After this *Prânâyâmic* preliminary comes the *mantra* for invoking the *Gâyatrî*. Sâyana says that this *mantra* for inviting *Gâyatrî* is to be repeated after sprinkling a little water on one's head. This *mantra* like many others that are used in Sandhyâ—

Vandana, occurs in the 10th Prapâthaka of the Taittiriya Aranyaka. It runs thus.

1. आयातु वरदा देवी अक्षरं ब्रह्मसम्मितम् ।
गायत्री छन्दसां माता इदं ब्रह्म जुषस्वनः* ।

2. ओजोऽसि सहोऽसि बलमसि भ्राजोऽसि देवानां धाम
नामासि विश्वमसि विश्वायुः सर्वमसि सर्वायुः अभिभूरों ।
गायत्रीमावाहयामि ॥ 26th Anuvaka.

1. Meaning. *Ayâtu* = may She come! *Varadâ Devi* = the Goddess who grants all our desires, understand *Uddis'ya* = for the purpose of making known to us, *Aksharam* = eternal, *Brahma* = the Supreme Source of the Universe, *Sammitam* = who is revealed to us through the Scriptures. *Gâyatrî* = (may) the Gâyatrî Devatâ, *Chhandasâm Mâtâ* = the Mother of all metres, or of all Vedas, *Jushasva* = *Joshayatu* = reveal, *Nah* = to us, *Idam Brahma* = the Eternal Truth.

May the Goddess *Gâyatrî Devatâ* who

---

* जुषस्वमे is another reading.

grants all our desires come to us to make known to us the Eternal Lord who is revealed to us only through the Scriptures*. May the Gâyatrì—the mother of all the Vedas—reveal to us the Eternal Truth!

Comment. There are hundreds of Vedic *Riks* in Gâyatrí metre; but it is the particular *Rik—Tat Savitur Varenyam &c.*—alone, that has come to be exclusively denoted by the term Gâyatrí. This prayer is thought to express, in the shortest possible compass, the entire teaching of the Vedas. Hence if in the entire body of Vedic revelation any one particular Rik is said to contain the spiritual essence of divine truth more than

* We have followed here as elsewhere the interpretation of Sâyana as found in his commentary on the Taittiriya Aranyaka. Narayana also proposes a slightly different interpretation thus: *Brahma Sammitam*=as exalted as the Vedas, and *Aksharam*=eternal, are both taken as epithets of *Devi*. *Idam Brahma Jushasva Nah* is taken by him to mean 'may she accept this prayer of ours!' The prayer is what follows.

any other, it is this prayer. Accordingly the Gâyatrî is regarded as the word of God *par excellence*, and (as the word Gâyatrî is of feminine gender in Sanskrit) is invoked as the Muse presiding over Divine Wisdom. The Gâyatrí is not to be approached in a light spirit of indifference or irreverence, but with true humility and sincere reverence in which frame of mind alone, Divine grace will enter and illumine our hearts; and the object of the invocation is to induce this reverential state of mind.

2. *Ojus—asi*=(Oh Gâyatri!) Thou art the source of all spiritual strength, *Sahas—asi*=Thou art the power that drivest away my enemies (*i.e.*, my evil inclinations); *Balam-asi*=Thou art the source of physical strength, *Bhrâjas—asi*=Thou art Divine Light, *Devânâm-dhâma-nâma-asi*=What light there is of the Gods, That thou art, *Vis'-vamasi*, *Sarvam—asi**=Thou art the entire

* Both mean the same.

Universe, *Vis'vâyuh—sarvâyuh—asi* = Thou art eternal, *Abhibhûh(asi)* = Thou causest the destruction of all sins. *Om* = Thou art the Pranava, *Gâyatrîm—âvâhayâmi* = I invoke (Thee) Gâyatri (of such powers).

Oh Gâyatri! Thou art the source of all spiritual strength. Thou art the power that drivest away the evil inclinations which are my enemies. Thou by conducing to a sound mind conducest to a sound body. Thou art the Light of the Gods that dispellest my intellectual darkness and illuminest my heart with divine wisdom. Thou art all. In the whole universe there is naught but Thee that *is*. Thou art the Eternal Truth that destroys all sins. Thou art the Pranava that reveals to me the Unknown. Come to my succour, Oh Thou Gâyatri! and make me wise.

Comment.—It is with thoughts like these and an implicit faith in the spiritual efficacy of the Gâyatrí that the worshipper should prepare to approach the Lord with the prayer of prayers. It is then that the heart is truly attuned to receive the divine light and the thoughts aroused by the Gâyatrí permeate the heart through and through and the worshipper exclaims in sincere devoutness, "Oh Lord! Thy glory is immense: Teach my heart to know Thee." When the heart of man is thus purged of all sinful thoughts and is taught to know God and love Him, earthly bonds begin to lose their power over the soul, and once it gets free of all corporeal ties, no power on earth is strong enough to attract it into mortal shackles again, and all that is said of Gâyatrì comes to be fulfilled.

After the invocation of the Gâyatrì comes the enumeration of the four principal characteristics of the Gâyatrí Rik. Every Rik has four marks (1) its *Rishi* or the seer* through whom the Rik was given

---

* The Rishi is not regarded by the orthodox as the

out to the world (2) its *Chhandas* or metre (3) its *Devata* or the Deity * whose praise it sings (4) its *Viniyoga* or the purpose to which the Rik is applied. When the name of the Rishi is mentioned, the worshipper touches his head and makes an *anjali* or obeisance in gratitude to the seer who has enriched the world with his inspired song. When its metre is mentioned, the worshipper touches his mouth with his right fingers to imply that the inspired

---

author of the Rik; for that would imply that the *mantra* is of human origin, whereas the *mantras* are supposed to be eternal and to have existed in the Lord and to have been *given out* to the world at some particular time through some sacred personage or Rishi who is supposed to have been simply the medium of divine communication. This is the orthodox view of the supernatural origin of the Vedas. Hence the saying

ऋषयो मन्त्रद्रष्टारः ।

* Sometimes the Rik is not a song in praise of any Deity, in which case the subject-matter of the Rik is spoken of as its Deity.

revelation came out of the mouth of the seer in that particular form and to request that he may be blessed with a flow of speech in reciting the mantra. When uttering the name of the Devata the worshipper touches his heart with his right fingers as much as to say that the Deity in whose honor the Rik is sung resides in his heart and to request that the Deity should be pleased to accept his prayer and the mention of the *Viniyoga* is to put him in mind of the object for which he prays.

These characteristics of Vedic Riks are recorded in the Anukramani or the explanatory Index of the Vedas and have since been extended to all *Bija* mantras. In the case of the Gâyatrî Rik, the Rishi is Vis'vâmitra, the *Chhandas* is of course Gâyatrî, the *Devatâ* is *Savitri*—not the sun but the Supreme Lord as we have elsewhere shown—and the *Viniyoga* or the purpose of the prayer is *Sâyujya* or absorption, through knowledge, into the Universal Soul. This last is borne out by the fact that the request made in the prayer is not for riches or 'our daily bread' but wisdom or knowledge of God.

Before the commencement of the Japam, two rituals called Anga Nyâsa and Kara Nyâsa are now generally performed. These are Tântric ceremonies—not Vaidic. Their importance is inculcated in Tântric works and directions for their *modus operandi* are given therein.

Kara Nyâsa.—The fingers are to be used in counting the repetitions of the Gâyatri; they have to be purified before they can be used for this purpose; so the worshipper says, अंगुष्ठाभ्यांनमः—*homage to the two thumbs;* तर्जनीभ्यां नमः—'*homage to the two fore-fingers,* मध्यमाभ्यां नमः—'*homage to the two middle fingers,*' अनामिकाभ्यां नमः—'*homage to the two nameless fingers*' (*i.e., the ring fingers*),

कनिष्ठिकाभ्यां नमः—'*homage to the two little fingers,*' करतलकरपृष्ठाभ्यां नमः—'*homage to the two palms and the two backs of the hands*'. As each of these pairs is named, it is touched. In Tântric Literature, it is supposed that the several parts of the body are sacred to particular deities and when a particular part of the body is named and touched, it is supposed to be an act of homage gratifying to the presiding deity of the part. The part thus consecrated becomes worthy of being used for sacred purposes.

Anga Nyâsa.—Each *Bîja mantra* is, in Tântric works, divided into six parts and each part is dedicated to the particular deity who is supposed to reside in a particular *Anga*. The first part of the Gâyatrî—तत्सवितुः—is held to be sacred to Brahma (of the Triad) who is supposed to reside in the heart: so the heart is touched and the worshipper says तत्सवितुः ब्रह्मात्मने हृदयाय नमः– 'homage to the heart whose presiding deity is Brahma, to whom I dedicate *Tatsavituh* the first part of the Gâyatri.' Next the head is touched with the prayer वरेण्यं विष्ण्वात्मने शिरसे स्वाहा—'homage to the head whose presiding deity is Vishnu, to whom I dedicate the second part *Varenyam*.' Then the top-knot is touched with the prayer भर्गोदेवस्य रुद्रात्मने शिखायैवषट्—'homage to the top-knot whose presiding deity is Rudra, to whom I dedicate the third part *Bhargodevasya*.' Next the two hands are crossed on the breast to represent a shield and the worshipper says धीमहि सत्यात्मने कवचायहुम् 'homage to the shield whose presiding deity is Satya to whom I dedicate the fourth part *Dhîmahi*.' Then the eyes are touched with the prayer धियोयोनः ज्ञानात्मनेनेत्रद्वयाय *वौ-

---

* नेत्रत्रयाय is another reading—the third eye being supposed to exist between the eye-brows and

षट्—'homage to the two eyes whose presiding deity is *Jnâna* to whom I dedicate the fifth part *Dhiyo—yo—nah.*' Lastly the right thumb and the right middle finger are snapped round the head. This act is supposed to represent a weapon and the mantra recited is प्रचोदयात् परमात्मने अस्त्राय-फट्— 'homage to the weapon whose presiding deity is Paramâtman, to whom I dedicate the last part *Prachodayât.*'

Brahma, Vishnu, Rudra, *Satya*, *Jnâna* and Paramâtman are not however distinct deities but are simply the various aspects of the one True God—Brahma representing the capacity of Creator, Vishnu that of Preserver, Rudra that of Destroyer, Satya Truth, the one immutable Being, Jnâna everlasting knowledge * and Para-

representing intellectual vision. This third eye or spiritual vision is allegorised by the third eye of Siva in later Pauranic Literature.

* Satya and Jnâna are supposed to be the forms of that formless Being.

mâtman the all-pervading Lord. Thus the dedication of the several parts to these several capacities of the same Supreme Being simply means that the whole Gâyatrí prayer is sacred to the Supreme Being and is directed to Him alone. The heart and the head, the first two *angas*, represent the seats of feeling and intellect respectively and imply that the *mantra* should be both *felt* and *understood*. The top-knot represents the halo of spirtual glory with which all deities are represented, as saints are in the Christian church, and symbolises the fact that the ultimate good resulting from the *mantra* is spiritual glory. The eyes of course imply that the *mantra* opens up the spiritual vision of the worshipper; the shield and the weapon imply that the *mantra* is able not only to protect him against evil thoughts when they come to tempt him but also to effectually destroy all evil thoughts and prevent them from ever arising in his mind.

All this may appear fantastic; but a close student of Indian Literature knows well enough that at one stage of Indian History when the springs of national life were sapped, the life-giving and soul-sustaining ideas of the national, mind were petrified into forms and symbols, and symbology took the place of philosophy. The *tantras* represent this morbid phase of Indian thought and hence often appear to the superficial reader crude and absurd, mysterious and fantastic. Yet, on a careful examination they will be found to represent, in a manner suited to the intellectual conditions of a deteriorated age, the older truths of Vedic theosophy. It is not to be understood that we have here taken up a brief for the Tantric Literature; but it is our conviction that the *tantras* can be rightly read only in the light of the foregoing remarks.

Then the Gâyatrì prayer is mentally repeated—generally 108 times. The worshipper concentrates his mind on the meaning of the prayer he utters, keeps his mind running on the thoughts evoked by the Gâyatrì and thinks of the supreme glory of the Divine Vivifier. The greater the number of repetitions of the Gâyatrî, the longer he thinks of the Lord and prays for divine wisdom, the more efficacious the prayer is considered to be. The object of the repetitions seems to be to only fix the minimum time during which the worshipper has to devote himself to the contemplation of the glory of the Lord.

During the repetition, the mind is easily kept from straying on other thoughts and the concentration thus induced leads ultimately to *Samâdhi*—an attitude in which all the organs, which, left to themselves run wild among ravishing sensualities, are controlled, and the mind, weaned away from all attachments to earthly things, becomes spiritualised. As the Manu Smriti puts it (II—96), 'the organs being strongly attached to sensual delights cannot so effectively be restrained by avoiding incentives to pleasure, as *by a constant* pursuit of divine knowledge.' Hence also 'the act of repeating His holy name is ten times better than the appointed sacrifice, a hundred times better when it is heard by no man, and a thousand times better when it is purely mental.' (Manu Smriti II 85).

This rational view of the matter will conflict with the preconceived notions of the orthodox section of our community. It is now generally believed that there is a mysterious efficacy in the particular collocation of the syllables which make up the *mantra*, that the mere utterance of the *mantra*, with or without a knowledge of its meaning, has the power to free one from all sins and confer all spiritual blessings.

Fire burns you if you touch it, whether you know it will burn you or not. Similarly the *mantra* has certain powers independent of your knowledge of its properties or meaning. This is the orthodox view of the question.

But it is easy to explain how such a belief has arisen. Throughout the Scriptures emphasis is laid on the importance of *knowledge.* Knowledge alone is said to confer supreme bliss. ब्रह्मैवसन् ब्रह्माप्येति यएवंवेद. Tait. Aran. 2. Prap 2. Anuvâka. Sâyana interprets it thus, प्राप्तात् वेदनात् अज्ञानापगमे सति स्वानुभवेनापि 'ब्रह्म' आप्नोति i. e. The worshipper secures beatific bliss through his spiritual experience when through *knowledge* his ignorance has been removed. Scores of references may be given but we think it needless. The Taittiriya Upanishad which forms the 7th, the 8th and the 9th Prapâthakas of the Taittiríya Aranyaka from which many of the Sandhyâ texts are taken insists on "the meditation of certain words which symbolically express the truth of the doctrine and prepare the mind for its comprehension, the meditation on the term '*Om*', the most sacred of all syllables, embracing as it does the real sense of the Vedas,—meditation on Brahman in His relation to the individual soul, to the material creation, and to the different deities, and the necessity of ceremonial work, of the daily reading of the Vedas, and of a virtuous life in accordance with the precepts of the S'astras." It inculcates these duties as *preparing the mind* for the reception of the highest knowledge.

But it was feared that a practice, however good, might come to be neglected by the people at large if special inducements were not offered to keep it up, and so supernatural rewards came to be attached to the performance of religious acts, and punishments, to their neglect. This bolstering up of a thing good in itself with adventitious aids is seen in many passsages of the Brâhmanas known as Arthavâda and forms, under the name Phalas'ruti, a leading feature of Puranic Literature. 'Gradually mysticism came to gain an ascendancy over the Indo-Aryan mind; the old speculations, rationalism, and freedom of thought in matters transcendental yielded to forms, set phrases, and mummery, and the religion of the ancient Aryan world disintegrated into the Tântric form of worship which now enthrals the religious instinct of the Hindu.'*

After the meditation on the meaning of the Gâyatrî, the worshipper sends back the Gâyatrì Devatâ to her place with the following *mantra* which forms the 30th Anuvâka of the 10th Prapâthaka of the Taittirîya Aranyaka.

---

* Dr. Rajendra Lal Mitra. Vide his edition of the Taitt. Aranyaka.

उत्तमे शिखरे देवी* भूम्यां पर्वतमूर्धनि ।
ब्राह्मणेभ्योऽभ्यनुज्ञाता† गच्छदेवि यथासुखम् ॥

Meaning:–*Devî* = The Goddess of Gâyatri, *Bhûmyâm* (having its base deeply fixed) in the earth, *Parvata-mûrdhani* = on the summit of the mountain (Meru), *Uttame Sikhare* = on the lofty peak, understand *Tishthati* = resides. Therefore, *Devi* = Oh Goddess. *Brâhmanebhyah* = from the Brahmans who worship Thee, *Abhyanugyâtâ* = taking leave, *Yathâ Sukham* = as it pleases Thee, *Gachchha* = go (to Thy abode in mount Meru).

The Goddess Gâyatrí resides on a lofty peak on the summit of mount Meru (whose base is deeply fixed) in the earth. Oh Thou Goddess, take leave from the Brahmans (who have worshipped Thee and who have been blessed with Thy grace) and go back

---

* Another reading जाते which means, Oh, Thou that art born.

† Do म्यनुज्ञानम्

to Thy abode as comfortably as possible.

Mount Meru is the Olympus of Hindu traditions. According to the Pauranic cosmogony, it is said to rise from the centre of the Jambu Dvípa, hence of the earth. All the planets are said to revolve round it. Its height is said to be 84,000 *yojanas,* 16,000 of which are below the surface of the earth. The river Ganges falls from heaven on its summit and flows thence to the surrounding worlds. The whole of it consists of gems and gold. It is considered to be the residence of all the gods; Satyaloka which is the residence of Brahma and his hosts, Vaikuntha the abode of Vishnu, and Kailasa of S'iva are all said to be situated on the various peaks of this mount. Gâyatrí Devatâ, representing as she does divine wisdom, is fitly regarded as residing with the gods on this mount and condescending to visit the heart of man if invoked with due humility.

Now comes the third division of the service, called the *Upasthâna*. The worshipper stands up and facing the sun prays to the Lord who is thought to reside in that luminary. But before he commences the *Upasthâna*, he contemplates the glory of the Divine Being with the following mantra which forms the 31st Anuvâka of the 10th Prap. of the Taitt. Aranyaka.

ओं अन्तश्चरति भूतेषु गुहायां विश्वमूर्तिषु ।
त्वं यज्ञस्त्वं विष्णुस्त्वं वषट्कारस्त्वं रुद्रस्त्वं ब्रह्मात्वं प्रजापतिः ॥

The Supreme Lord symbolised by *Om* dwells within the mind of all the created beings of the Universe. Oh Lord! Thou art sacrifice, Thou art Vishnu the preserver, Thou art Vashatkâra, the mantra for offering oblations, Thou art Rudra the destroyer, Thou art Brahma the creator, Thou art Prajâpati, the ruler of men. This *mantra* is repeated here to prevent him from forgetting that all this adoration is directed to the nameless One symbolised by the Pranava, who takes various names as He is regarded in various aspects.

The hymns invoking the rising sun in the morning form the closing mantras of the fourth *Pras'na* of the third Kânda of the Taittiriya Samhita. They are also found with some slight variations in the fourth Adhyâya of the third Ashtaka of the Rig Veda. They run thus:—

1. मित्रस्य चर्षणी धृतः श्रवोदेवस्य सानसिम् । सत्यं चित्रश्रवस्तमम् ।

2. मित्रोजनान् यातयतिप्रजानन्मित्रोदाधारपृथिवीमुतद्याम् । मित्रः कृष्टीरनिमिषाभिचष्टेसत्यायहव्यं घृतवद्विधेम ।

3. प्रसमित्रमर्तोअस्तु प्रयस्वान् यस्त आदित्य शिक्षतिव्रतेन । नहन्यतेनजीयतेत्वोतोनैनम*हो अश्नोत्यन्तितोनदूरात् ।

Meaning :—*Charshanidhritah* = protecting men (by causing rain), *Mitrasya Devasya* = of the sun god, *S'ravah* = glory, **Sânasim*

---

* The Rig Veda reading *Sânasi* (in the N. Nom. case)

=*Sambhâjaniyam*=adorable, *Satyam*=real and everlasting, *Chitras'ravastamam*=and most worthy of being adored with wonder; understand 'we sing.'

(2) *Mitrah*=The sun, *Prajânan*=well-knowing (the inclinations and pursuits of several men)*Janân*=men, *Vâtayati*=directs (to their several pursuits); *Mitrah*=The sun, *Prithivîm*=the earth,*Uta*=and, *Dyâm*=the heaven, *Dâdhâra*=upholds; *Mitrah*=the sun, *Animishâ*=without winking (i. e. incessantly) *Krishtîh*=men, *Abhichashte*=*Sarvatah Pas'yati*=is observing everywhere; *Satyâya*=to this Eternal Being; *Ghritavat-havyam*=the oblations mixed with ghee, *Vidhema*=we offer.

(3) *Aditya*=Oh sun, *Yah*=who,*Vratena* =through (such) sacrifice, *Te*=to thee,

---

makes better sense. We need not as in the Taittiriya text take the *rik* elliptically. According to the Rig Veda reading, it means—'The glory of the sun god who sustains all men is adorable; that glory is eternal and most worthy of being adored with wonder.

S'ikshati = offers oblations, *Sah Martah* = that man, *Mitra* = Oh sun, *Prayasvân* = endowed with food (and plenty), *Prâstu* = *Prabhavatu* = let him become;

Tva Utah=He who is protected by you, *Nahanyate*=is not cut off by (untimely death), *Najîyate*=is not vanquished (by anybody), *Amhas*=sin, *Yenam*=this man, *Na As'noti*= does not take hold of, *Antitah*=near, *Na Dûrât*=not far.

1. (We sing) the adorable glory of the sun god, who sustains all men (by causing rain), which glory is eternal and most worthy of being adored with wonder.

2. The sun well knowing the inclinations of several men directs them to their several pursuits; the sun upholds both heaven and earth; the sun observes all creatures (and their actions) without ever winking; to this eternal Being we offer the oblation mixed with clarified butter.

3. Oh sun! may that man who through

such sacrifice offers oblations to thee become endowed with wealth and plenty; (for) he who is under thy protection is not cut off by untimely death; he is not vanquished by any body and sin has no hold on this man either from near or from afar.

Comment. 1. Three things are implied in the foregoing prayer: i. The mind of the worshipper should contemplate with wonder and reverence, the supreme glory of the Lord. ii. He should extol His glory in songs. iii. And he should offer oblations to Him; thus worshipping Him through mind, word, and deed—(*Manasâ Vâchâ Karmanâ.*)

2. Prominence is given to the idea that nothing escapes the eye of the Lord,

"Who sees with equal eye, as God of all,
A hero perish or a sparrow fall,
Atoms or systems into ruin hurl'd,
And now a bubble burst and now a world,"

that man by himself is powerless; that he

even does as he is directed by the supreme Lord, that through His divine grace alone man can hope to crush all evil thoughts, and triumph over *sin* and Death.

3. Sin *either from near or from far* has no hold on him. The expression *sin either from near or from far*, if it is to have any meaning, must be interpreted to mean 'sins of present birth or sins of former births.' Sâyana, it must be admitted, does not offer this interpretation; but both Haradatta and Nârâyana do. Sâyana has passed over this passage, simply remarking that *Antitah* means *Samîpât*. Western scholars have remarked that the songs of the Rig Veda do not seem to know the theory of several births, which occupies such a prominent place in the philosophy of the Upanishads, which we find there so elaborated and perfected and whose developments we see in later works like Manu Smriti. But Dr. Weber himself is of

opinion that the doctrine of the transmigration of souls as enunciated in the Chhandogya and other Upanishads is found there in such a complete form as to make it certain that it existed long before the date of these treatises. Is it then unreasonable to surmise that in passages like these we discern glimpses of the doctrine of re-birth? The first Rik of the 89th Sûkta of the VII Mandala of the Rig Veda has in our opinion clear reference to this theory. It runs thus :—

मोषुवरुणमृन्मयं गृहं राजन्नहंगमम्। मृळासुक्षत्रमृळय ॥

According to Sâyana's interpretation "Oh Lord Varuna, let me not obtain the house of clay (which I now have); Oh thou of shining wealth, make me happy; have mercy on me."

This passage clearly shows that the worshipper is afraid of again entering the house of clay (i. e. the mortal body), that happiness consists in freedom from rebirth and that such happiness can be secured only through the grace of the Lord.

4. Mitra is invoked in the morning and Varuna in the evening. Mitra represents the rising sun and Varuna the evening sky and are apt symbols of the Supreme Being in the morning and the evening twilight.

The Texts recited during the mid-day *Upashthâna* are taken from the Tattirîya Samhita, and the Taittirîya Aranyaka. They are also found with some slight variations in the first *Mandala* of the Rig Veda.

1. आसत्येन रजसा वर्तमानोनिवेशयन्नमृतं मर्त्यंच । हिरण्ययेनसवितारथेनदेवोयातिभुवनाविपश्यन् ॥ T.S.3.5.

2. उद्वयं तमसस्परि पश्यन्तो ज्योतिरुत्तरम् । देवं देवत्रासूर्यमगन्मज्योतिरुत्तमम् ॥ T. S. 4. I. 7.

3. उदुत्यं जातवेदसं देवं वहन्ति केतवः । दृशेविश्वायसूर्यम् । चित्रं देवानामुदगादनीकं चक्षुर्मित्रस्य वरुणस्याग्नेः । आप्राद्यावा पृथिवी अन्तरिक्ष सूर्य आत्मा जगतस्तस्थुषश्च ॥ T. S. 1. 4. 4. 3.

4. तच्चक्षुर्देवहितं पुरस्ताच्छुक्रमुच्चरत् । पश्येम शरदः शतं जीवेम शरदः शतं नन्दाम शरदः शतं मोदाम शरदः शतं भवाम शरदः शतं शृणवाम शरदः शतं प्रब्रवाम शरदः शतमजीताः स्याम शरदः शतं ज्योक्च सूर्यं दृशे । य उदगान्महतोऽर्णवाद्विभ्राजमानः सरिरस्य मध्यात् समा वृषभो लोहिताक्षः सूर्यो विपश्चिन्मनसा पुनातु ॥

Tait. Aran. 4th Prap.24 An.

1. *Satyenarajasâ**=Through the *Satyaloka* i.e. through the heavens, *Avartamânah*=repeatedly appearing, *Amritam*†=god, *Mar-*

---

* The Rig Veda reading is आकृष्णेन रजसा (1. 35)

कृष्णवर्णेन लोकेन=अन्तरिक्षमार्गेण

Rajas=world (Yâska).

† Sâyana proposes another interpretation thus:—

Amritam=deathless life, *Martyancha*=and mortal body, *Niveśayan*=bestowing (on men, according to the nature of their deeds on earth), i.e., granting to men eternal life or a mortal body according to their deeds on earth. If this be the correct interpretation *tyamcha*=and man, *Nives'ayan*=sustaining in their several stations, *Savitâ Devah*=the sun god, *Bhuvanâ Vipas'yan**=beholding i.e. illuminating all the worlds, *Hiranyayena Rathena*=in a golden chariot; *Yâti*=comes (near us.)

The Lord Savitâ daily appears in the heavens; he sustains gods and men; (or he confers on men eternal bliss or a mortal body once more according as they acquit themselves on earth); he comes in a golden chariot, illuminating all the worlds:—

2. *Vayam*=we (the worshippers), *Tamasuspari*=above the darkness (of night) or (resting) above sin, *Uttaram Jyotis*=the loftier light, *Devatra Devam*=God among the gods, *Sûryam*=the sun, *Utpas'yantah*=looking upon (i.e. adoring with offerings), *Utta-*

(and Sâyana evidently prefers this meaning) we have here another passage which contains a reference to the doctrine of transmigration.

* The Rig Veda reading is *Bhuvanâni pas'yan.*

mam Jyotis=the most excellent Light, *Aganma*=attain.

Adoring the sun, God among the gods, the loftier light that rests above darkness or sin, we attain (beatific union with that) most excellent Light.

The earliest comment on this *rik*, that which is separated from it by the shortest possible interval, is to be found in the Taittirîya Samhita and it is a very interesting comment in more ways than one. It runs thus;—

तमसस्परीत्याह पाप्मा वै तमः पाप्मानमेवास्मादपहन्ति ।
अगन्मज्योतिरुत्तममित्याहासौ वा आदित्यः ज्योतिरुत्तममादित्यस्यैव सायुज्यं गच्छति ॥

This passage may be freely rendered thus;

Tamas is sin and Sûrya is said to be *Tamasas Pari* (above sin), because he absolves us (the worshippers) of all sins. The worshipper is said to attain the most excellent Light because he attains *Sâyujya* with the sun.

This passage thus implies (1) that the sincere worshipper is absolved of all his sins through the grace of the *God among the gods*; (2) and that he, being thus freed from all taint of sin, becomes one with the supreme Light i.e., is emancipated from all earthly trammels (after he has shuffled off his mortal coil) and is absorbed into the divine Essence. *Sâyujya* is a technical term applied in the later schools of philosophy to the doctrine of 'Final absorption into divine essence', and it is instructive to note that the earliest and the most reliable interpretation of the *Rik* bears clear reference to one of the most advanced theories developed by S'amkara. Let us not forget that this interpretation is to be found in a *Samhita* and that, the *Taittirîya* Samhita, the compilation of which is, by the general *consensus* of orthodox opinion, attributed to Krishna Dvaipâyana Vyâsa and assigned to a period of time immediately preceding the commencement of the Kaliyuga which, in the absence of any *conclusive* evidence to the contary, we have to place at about 3101 B. C.

3. *Ketavah*=the horses (or the rays), *Udvahanti*=bear aloft, *Tyam*=*Prasiddham*= glorious, *Sûryam Devam*=sun god, *Jâtavedasam*=*Jâtânâm Veditâram*=who knows all that lives, (or the source of knowledge or wealth) *Vis'vâya Dris'e*=that all may look on Him.

His steeds or rays bear him aloft, the God who knows the ways of all living beings, Sûrya, that all may look on him (and adore him and become wise).

4. *Devânâm*=of the rays, *Chitram*= wonderful, *Anîkam*=collection, *Udagât*=has risen, *Mitrasya, Varunasya, Agneh*=of Mitra, Varuna and Agni (i.e., of earth, air and the heavens presided over by these deities), *Chakshus*=the eye, *Dyâvâprithivî*=the earth and the heavens, *Antariksham*=(and) the sky,

Aprâh=has filled with his light; *Sûryah*= This Sûrya, *Atmâ*=(is) the soul, *Jagatah*=of all that moves, *Tasthushascha*=and of all that moves not.

The wonderful collection of rays (the orb of light) has risen; this orb is the eye of the earth, air and heaven; this orb has filled the earth, air and heaven with light, everywhere. Sûrya (the Lord that resides in this orb) is the soul of all things that move and all that move not.

(1) Mr. Griffiths translates *Devânâm Anîkam* into 'the presence of the Gods'; but Sâyana evidently prefers the meaning we have given; he says दीव्यन्तीतिदेवाः रश्मयः. He also says *Devânâm* may be taken to mean *Devajanânâm*; but in the sequal he sticks to his first interpretation. Also in the 13th Anuvâka of the 2nd Prapâthaka of the Taittirîya Aranyaka where the same verse is mentioned, *Devânâm* is taken in the sense of दीप्यमानानां रश्मीनाम् alone and *Chitram*

is taken to mean 'of various colours.' The expression 'presence of the gods' hardly makes sense as applied to Sûrya.

(2) Sûrya is the soul of all that moves and moves not. Sâyana interprets this passage in two ways:—(i) Sûrya is the universal Paramâtman who resides as *Antaryâmin* in all living beings and directs them. In his commentary on this *rik*, in the Taittirìya Aranyaka, Sâyana interprets it to mean 'The Paramâtman who resides as Súrya in the orb of light also lives as Jívâtman in all living beings.'

(ii) The sun is the source of all life and activity or as the Taitt. Aranyaka puts it so beautifully: "The sun rises bringing back with him the lives of all living beings that are buried during night in sleep—'twin brother to Death'."

We have seen in more places than one that some of the more advanced doctrines of philosophy are to be met with in the hymns of the Rig Veda and it will be difficult for western *savants* to convince the orthodox pandits that the doctrines of Vedantic philosophy were unknown to the sages of the earliest period.

5. *Tat*=that (well-known), *Chakshus*=eye, (i.e. orb of the sun), *Devahitam*=that does good to the Devas, *Sukram*=brilliant, *Purastât*=in the east, *Uchcharat*=rises; *Saradah Satam*=for a hundred autumns, (this phrase is to be repeated before every one of the verbs that follow), *Pas'yema*=may we see (this orb), *Nandâma*=may we live in plenty (through his grace), *Modâma*=may we be happy, *Bhavâma*=may we live secure in our places, *Srinavâma*=may we learn the secrets of Vedic truths from our teachers, *Prabravâma*=may we impart these truths to our disciples, *Ajîtâsyâma*=may we be never defeated, *Cha*=and, *Jyok*=for a long time, *Sûryam Dris'e*=(may we be able) to see the sun.

This brilliant eye, the orb of the sun, on whom as Lord of the sacrifices, the Devas depend for their oblations, rises in the east. May we live a hundred years to see him, may we live in plenty through his grace, may we be happy in his presence for a hundred years, may we, through his grace, live secure in our homes, may we learn the secrets of Vedic theosophy from our Achâryas, and may we gladly impart the same to our disciples, may we never meet with reverses, and may we long live to see and adore the sun!

6. *Yah*=who, *Mahatah—arnavât*=from the great (Eastern ocean), *Udayât*=rises, *Sarirasya—madhyât*=from the midst of waters, *Vibhrâjamânah*=with resplendent glory; *Sah*=he, *Vrishabhah*=he who showers wealth and all other blessing, *Lohitâkshah*=he who is red-eyed, *Vipaschit*=all-wise, *Mâ*=me, *Manasâ*=by mind, *Punâtu*=may he make pure.

May he who rises with resplendent glory from the midst of waters, out of the Eastern ocean—the bright-eyed and all-wise *Sûrya* who showers all blessings (on his worshippers)—may he make me pure in mind!

The *mantras* for the evening Upasthâna are taken from the second and the third Kândas of the Tait. Samhita. They are also found in the second Adhyâya of the first Ashtaka of the Rig Veda. They run thus;—

1. इमंमेवरुणश्रुधीहवमद्याचमृडय । त्वामवस्युराचके ।
2. तत्वायामि ब्रह्मणावन्दमानस्तदाशास्ते यजमानोहविर्भिः ।
अहेडमानोवरुणेहबोध्युरुशꣳ समानआयुः प्रमोषीः ॥

T. S. 2...I–last Anuvâka.

3. यच्चिद्धिते विशोयथाप्रदेववरुणव्रतम् । मिनीमसिद्यविद्य-
वि ।
4. यत्किंचेदंवरुणदैव्ये जनेभिद्रोहंमनुष्याश्चरामसि । अचि-
त्ती यत्तव धर्मायुयोपिममानस्तस्मादेनसोदेवरीरिषः ।
5. कितवासो यद्रिरिपुर्नदिवियद्वाघासत्यमुतयन्नविद्म ।

सत्राँतात्रिष्ये शिथिरेवं देवार्थातेस्यामवरुणाप्रियासः ॥

T. S. 3. 4. last Anu.

1. *Varuna*=Oh Varuna ! *Me*=my, *Imam* =this, *Havam*=invocation, *Srudhi*=hear, *Cha* =and, *Adya*=to-day, *Mridaya*=make (me) happy, *Avasyuh*=longing for thy protection, *Tvâm*=thee, *Achake*=I cry (i.e. praise).

Hear, Oh Vâruna, this prayer of mine; be gracious unto me this day; longing for thy protection I cry to thee.

These *riks* are said to have been taught by Vis'vâmitra to *Sunassephah* when he was tied to the sacrificial post and about to be immolated by Harischandra to appease the wrath of Varuna. The prayer saved him. (Vide Ait. Brah).

Western scholars are of opinion that in Varuna the ancient Indo-Aryans gave expression to the most sublime conception of the Supreme Being. Professor Max Müller says in his 'Chips from a German Workshop' Vol. II: "Uranus is the Sanskrit Varuna;

and derived from a root *Var* to cover ; Varuna being in the Veda also a name of the firmament, but especially connected with the night and opposed to Mitra the day."

The spacious firmament on high, the spangled heavens, the starry blue 'thick inlaid with bright patins of gold' proclaim as with a voice of trumpet, their Great Original, whose wish has called them into existence, and by whose immutable laws (*vritas*) the moon moves on in splendour, and the twinkling stars have their rising and setting. It is this sublime aspect of nature (and who that has seen it, has not felt it ?) that has given birth to the most exalted conception of God in the Vedas as later in the Zendavesta,* and accordingly we find

* The late lamented Prof. J. Darmestater says that the Sovereign God of Persia can be recognised as God of the heavens. 'The ancient formulæ of the Zoroastrian litanies say that the sun is His eye and the sky is the garment embroidered with stars, with which He arrays Himself. Like Varuna, like Zeus, lightning is in His hands.'

Varuna described in the Vedas as having the sun for his eye, the heaven for his garment and the resounding wind for his breath. He has lifted on high the bright and glorious heaven; he has stretched out the starry sky and the earth. The twinkling stars, the lovely moon with whose flood of light all heaven overflows, the peace and calmness that everywhere pervade nature at night induce a corresponding harmony in the soul of man and the contrite sinner thinks of his littleness and the Creator's greatness and he prays for forgiveness and mercy. It is thus to Varuna that some of the most touching appeals for mercy are preferred.

To suppose then, as some western scholars do, that Varuna represents the material sky would be confounding cause with effect and would be doing injustice to one of the most poetic Vedic conceptions of the Ruler of the Universe. The foregoing remarks will explain why the Supreme Being is invoked as Varuna in the evening *Upasthána.*

2. *Brahmaná*=with prayer, *Vandamánah*= adoring (thee), *Tat*=that (i.e. long life), *Tvâ*= (of) thee, *Yâmi*=beg; *Yajamânah*=the sacrificer, *Havirbhih*=with oblations, *Tat*=that (i.e. long life), *As'âste*=prays for; (therefore) *Varuna*=Oh Varuna! *Ahedamânah*= without indifference, *Iha*=here, *Bodhi*=know (i.e. take my prayer into your consideration), *Urus'amsa*=Oh thou that art adored by many, *Nah Ayus*=our life, *Mâ Pramoshîh*=do not take away.

Adoring thee with prayer, I beg long life of thee; the sacrificer does the same with the oblations he offers thee; therefore, Oh Varuna! without indifference in this matter, take my prayer into your kind consideration and do not cut off our life.

3. *Deva Varuna*=Oh Lord Varuna! *Yachchid Hi*=whatever, *Te Vratam*=law of thine, *Dyavi Dyavi*=day after day, *Praminî-*

*masi** = we violate, *Vis'ah Yathâ* = as men, (understand ' forgive us the trespasses'.)

Oh Lord Varuna! Whatever law of thine we, as men, violate day after day, forgive us those trespasses.

The ethical consciousness of human frailty and the appeal for mercy and forgiveness based on such consciousness find a beautifully simple and earnest expression in this Rik and the following.

4. *Varuna* = Oh Lord Varuna! *Dairye Jane* = *Deva Samuharupe Jane* = against all divine beings, *Yad Kimcha Idam* = whatever this, *Abhidroham* = offence, *Manushyâs* = as men, *Chardmasi** = we commit, *Achitti* = Achityâ = through ignorance, *Yat Tava Dharma* = whatever work of thine, *Yuyopima* = we have neglected, *Deva* = Oh Lord, *Tasmât Enasah* = for that sin, *Nah* = us, *Ma Ririshas* = do not destroy.

---

* The modern forms are *minimas*; and *charâmas*, the vowel being affixed in Vedic forms according to the Sûtra of Panini— इदम् तो मसिः

Oh Lord Varuna, whatever offence we, as men, have committed against divine beings, whatever work of thine we have neglected through ignorance, do not destroy us, Oh Lord, for such sin.

5. *Yat*=what offence, *Nadivi**=as in gambling, *Kitavâsah*‡=gamblers, so our enemies, *Riripuh*=have attributed (to us), *Va*=or, *Ghâ* is an expletive, *Yat Satyam*= what (sin we have) really (committed), *Uta* =and, *Yat Na Vidma*=what (sin we have committed) without knowing, *Sarvâ Tâ*= *Sarvâni Tâni*=all that, *Sithireva*=as scattered, *Vishya*=destroy, *Deva*=Oh Lord, *Atha*=then, *Te*=of thee, *Priyâsah*‡ = beloved, *Syâma*=we shall become.

Whatever offence is attributed to us by our enemies as by gamblers àt dice, whatever sins we may have really committed and

---

* *Na* is here used in *Upamârtha* and means 'just as.'

‡ *Kitavâsah* and *Priyâsah* are the Vedic forms of *Kitavâh* and *Priyâh*.

what we may have done without knowing, do thou scatter and destroy all those sins; then, Oh Lord, we shall become beloved of thee.

We may compare this with the 6th Rik of the 86th Súkta of the VII Mandala which says: 'Oh Varuna, all this sin is not wilfully committed by us; error or wine, dice or ignorance has given birth to our sin.'

The Rigvedins recite the *mantra*, *Uttame &c.*, at the close of the service. After the *Gâyatrî Japam*, they recite the *Upasthâna mantra*; the *mantra* for the morning and the evening is the same with them. It is as follows.

1. जातवेदसे सुनवामसोममरातीयतो निदहाति वेदः ।
सनः पर्षदति दुर्गाणि विश्वा नावेव सिन्धुं दुरितात्यग्निः ॥
R. V. I—99—1.

We offer the *soma* libation to Agni who knows all things that have been born: may he destroy the wealth of him who acts as our enemy! May he enable us to cross over all ills as we cross over the sea with a ship! May Agni enable us to get over (all sins which are the sources of sorrow!)

2. तच्छं यो रा वृणीमहे । गातुं यज्ञार्य ।
गातुं यज्ञ पतये । दैवी स्वस्तिरस्तुनः ।
स्वस्ति मानुषेभ्यः । ऊर्ध्वं जिगातु भेषजं ।
शन्नो अस्तु द्विपदे । शं चतुष्पदे ।.

We pray for the assuagement of ills that exist and for blessings; so that we may chant in praise of sacrifice, chant in praise of the Lord of sacrifices. May divine blessings come to us! May blessings come to all men! May healing medicaments be over (us)! May health attend on our two footed (sons, relatives and servants)! May health attend on our four-footed (cows &c)!

3. नमो ब्रह्मणे नमो अस्त्वग्नये नमः पृथिव्यै नम ओषधीभ्यः । नमो वाचे नमो वाचस्पतये नमो विष्णवे बृहते करोमि ॥

Salutation to Brahman, salutation be to Agni, salutation to the earth, salutation to the plants, salutation to speech, salutation to the Lord of speech. I offer salutation to the great Vishnu.

At noon the Rigvedins perform the *Upasthâna* before *Japam*. This *Upasthâna mantra* is the 50th *Sûkta* of the first Mandala.

1. उदु त्यं जातवेदसं देवं वहन्ति केतवः । दृशे विश्वाय सूर्यं ॥

His steeds bear him aloft,—the God who knows the ways of all living beings—Sûrya, that all may look on him.

2. अप त्ये तायवो यथा नक्षत्रा यन्त्यक्तुभिः । सूराय विश्वचक्षसे ॥

(Afraid) of the (rising) sun, who is the eye of all the Universe, the stars fly away with the night as notorious robbers (fly away at the sight of pursuers).

3. अदृश्रमस्य केतवो वि रश्मयो जनाँ अनु । भ्राजन्तो अग्नयो यथा ॥

His bright rays look on all men (*i.e.* illumine the whole universe) like shining fires.

4. तरणिर्विश्वदर्शतो ज्योतिष्कृदसि सूर्य । विश्वमाभासि रोचनम् ॥

Oh Sûrya, thou traversest the heavens, thou art to be seen by all, thou art the source of all light, thou illuminest the expansive sky.

Sâyana offers a Vedantic interpretation also.

5. प्रत्यङ्‌ देवानां विशः प्रत्यङ्ङुदेषि मानुषान् । प्रत्यङ्‌विश्वं स्वर्दृशे ॥

Thou risest so that the *Maruts* may behold thee before them, that men may see thee, that thou may illumine the abode of the Gods.

6. येना पावक चक्षसा भुरण्यन्तं जना॑ऽ अनु । त्वं वरुण पश्यसि ॥

Oh purifier, oh Varuna (*i.e.* Sûrya), with

what eye thou beholdest this world which sustains all men, (I praise that eye or light).

7. विद्योमैषि रजस्पृथ्वहा मिमानो अक्तुभिः । पश्यञ्जन्मानिसूर्य ॥

Oh Súrya, thou traversest the spacious expanse of the firmament, causing day with night and beholding all things born.

8. सप्तत्वा हरितो रथे वहन्ति देवसूर्य । शोचिष्केशं विचक्षण ॥

Oh Lord Súrya that illuminest all, seven steeds bear thee in a car—thee whose hair is thy rays.

9. अयुक्त सप्त शुन्ध्युवः सूरोरथस्यनप्त्यः । ताभिर्याति स्वयुक्तिभिः ॥

Súrya has yoked the seven mares who draw the car without upsetting it. With these self-yoked mares does he come (to receive our worship).

10. उद्वयं तमसस्परि ज्योतिष्पश्यन्त उत्तरं । देवं देवत्रा सूर्य मगन्म ज्योतिरुत्तमम् ॥

Adoring the sun, God among the gods, the loftier light that rests above darkness or sin, we attain (beatific union with) that most excellent Light.

11. उद्यन्नद्य मित्रमह आरोहन्नुत्तरां दिवं ।
हृद्रोगंमम सूर्य हरिमाणं च नाशय ॥

Oh thou Sûrya of friendly rays, gloriously rising and ascending the heavens, do thou destroy all my ills, bodily and mental.

12. शुकेषु मे हरिमाणं रोपणाकासुदध्मसि ।
अथोहारिद्रवेषु मे हरिमाणं निदध्मसि ॥

We transfer our pale yellow colour (due to Jaundice and other diseases) to parrots, and *Sârikas*, and to the *Haritâla* trees.

13. उदगादयमादित्यो विश्वेन सहसा सह ।
द्विषन्तं मह्यं रन्धयन्मो अहं द्विषतेरधं ॥

The sun hath risen with all his strength, destroying the (disease) that oppresses me; I need not (therefore) harm my enemy (the disease).

Some Rigvedins recite in addition to this hymn the 115th Súkta of the first Mandala and the last rik of the 36th Sùkta, X Mandala. But these are not mentioned in the Rigvedic *Ahnika*.

They then perform the Gâyatrí *Japam* and afterwards send back the *Gâyatrî Devatâ* with the *mantra*, *Uttame* &c.

The Sâmavedins, after sending back the *Gâyatrî Devatâ* directly offer salutation to the several directions without *Upasthâna*. Some, however, recite the following *Upasthâna mantra* in the morning.

अच्छिद्रां पारयिष्णुं शतारित्रां स्वस्तये। नम आदित्याय।
उद्यन्तं त्वादित्य अनु दियासं॥

In the evening the closing portion of this *mantra* उद्यन्तं &c is changed into

प्रतितिष्ठन्तं त्वादित्यानु प्रतितिष्ठासं.

Oh sun, thou (ascendest the ship) which is not leaky, which is able to take thee over to the (other) shore (of the ocean of the sky) and which has a hundred oars, for the well-being (of us all). I have followed thee who hast risen (or turned back with thee that hast turned back—this in the evening.)

नमः आदित्याय.

Salutation to the sun.

At noon the Sâmavedins have this Upasthana *mantra*—the third mid-day Upasthana *mantra* of the Yajurvedins. (Tait. Sam. I, 4, 4, 3, explained above); then they recite the following.

सूर्य इव दृशे भूयासं । अग्निरिव तेजसा । वायुरिव प्राणेन । सोम इव गन्धेन । बृहस्पतिरिव बुद्ध्या । अश्विनाविव रूपेण । इन्द्राग्नी इव बलेन । ब्रह्मभाग एवाहं भूयासं । पाप्म भागामे द्विषन्तः ॥

May I be like the sun in sight, like Agni in lustre, like Vâyu in life, like Soma in fragrance, like Brihaspati in intellect, like the As'vins in form, like Indra and Agni in strength! May I share in Brahman alone! May my enemies share my sins!

After the *Upasthâna*, the worshipper pays his obeisance to the gods residing in all the directions and says प्राच्यै दिशेनमः याश्चदेवता एतस्यां प्रतिवसन्ति एताभ्यश्चनमः Salutation to the East and the gods residing in that direction and so on to the south, the west, the north, the upper and the lower regions.

Then he says कामोकार्षीन्मन्युरकार्षीन्नमो नमः— 'What sin I have committed, that passion has done, that anger has done'.

The *Sandhyâ* prayer now closes with the *Abhivâdana* or salutation; but many Brahmans are in the habit of reciting at this stage a few *slokas* in praise of Vishnu and other deities of the Puranic Pantheon. These *slokas* do not form an integral part of the Vedic *Sandhyâ* ceremony and they differ according to the predilections of the worshipper.

The *Abhivâdana* runs in this form: अभिवादये........प्रवरान्वित........गोत्रः........शाखाध्यायी.....

...,...,...,सूत्रः............शर्माहं अस्मिभो ॥

I, born in the family of such and such a *Rishi*, which possesses such and such a line of progenitors, a student of such and such a Veda and a follower of such and such a Sûtra, by name so and so, salute thee.

A Brahman tags to his name, the title *s'arman*, a Kshatriya *varman*, and a Vaisya *gupta*. The whole ceremony is brought to a close by an internal purification of the body by *Achamana* and dedicating the entire service gone through to Parabrahman.

We will now close this survey of *Sandhyâvandanam* with a few concluding observations. Our readers will have seen that the *Sandhyâ* service is simply a thanksgiving and a prayer to the Universal Father. It begins with the external purification of the body by sprinkling water over the head and reciting a few hymns in praise of water and an internal purification by sipping a few drops of water and praying that all the sins committed during the preceding twelve hours be washed away. After having thus purified himself externally and internally the worshipper feels that he is worthy of approaching the Supreme Lord and pays his adorations to Him by the offering of water according to the immemorial usage of the Brahmans. He looks at the sun and makes his offering. It is not, however, to the sun but to the nameless One that he offers his simple tribute. But the sun is the visible symbol of God's power and glory, and when he rises in the heavens and brightens hill and dale with his golden rays or goes down the horizon leaving behind him a rich, though short-lived, legacy of crimson brilliance, he seems to speak directly to our heart and bid us praise the Lord whose will has breathed into him all the glory and effulgence; and the worshipper, in heartfelt obedience to this eloquent call offers his humble greetings to the glorious Father. Then he shuts his eyes and contemplates His glory and prays for *wisdom* that he might know Him and love Him and have Him. Then he stands up and sings His praises with Vedic hymns and implores Him to forgive him his sins and vouchsafe to him His grace and blessings.

This then is the aim of the *Sandhyâ* service. We have, in the preceding pages, tried to show that it is not to this or that aspect of nature that the worship is directed but to Him alone, whose phenomenal manifestation all nature is. The Vedic hymns and *Mantras* used in the service may have perhaps, as western scholars think, been directed to nature worship, though, for our part, we fail to see how the same Vedic Rishis who have given us, in some of their sublime out-bursts, the most exalted conceptions of the Infinite could have been so foolish as to mistake life-less nature for the living life behind. But the Brâhmanas and Aranyakas furnish incontestable evidence to the fact that in the *Sandhyâ* service at any rate, these hymns and *mantras* were referred to the Supreme Lord alone.

The service is entirely Vedic ; but later ages have made many additions to it in the shape of thanks-giving *slokas* from the Puranas. These later and superfluous additions we have purposely omitted as tending to adulterate the Vedic essence; and as likely to scare away, by its very bulk, those who may otherwise be disposed to look on it with favour. We have pointed out what constitutes the essence of the ceremony and its spirit. We leave it to our readers to judge of its utility and spiritual efficacy.

We have insisted on the necessity of a knowledge of the meaning of the *mantras* used. In this respect we may have perhaps departed from the orthodox view which holds that the rite has its own value whether performed knowingly or otherwise. It is indeed a wise provision to insist on the performance of the ceremony with or without a knowledge of its significance. Otherwise people who have hardly time, much less the inclination, for a study that does not hold out any immediate tangible inducements, may be led to neglect the rite altogether in favour of more useful (!), that is, money-making avocations, and the institution of *Sandhyá* service would have become defunct. But a prayer that appeals to the mercy of God is nothing if it does not come from the heart and it has very little chance of coming from the heart if it is recited in a mechanical, parrot-like sort of way. The Aranyakas have recognized this fact and many texts may be quoted therefrom to show that mechanical recitation is next to useless. We might even go further and say that it is a profane travesty of a sacred function. The *mantras* are praise and prayer; and when we are at this solemn duty, let us know what we are about, let us know what we are praying for; let us know Whom we praise and how, and let us approach Him with noble words nobly uttered. Let us not mouth the sublime language as your town-criers do, reckless of accent and intonation, but let us recognize the solemnity of the occasion and speak to Him in the noble language of our ancient fathers, in those solemn tones which, as they fall so melodiously on our ears, attune our souls to the sublime cadence and induce an attitude of mind that harmonises with the sentiments on our lips.

And is this asking too much? The *Sandhyávandanam* is one of the few remaining links that unite us to a glorious past. It is a link that may not be rudely snapped asunder. It is a duty rendered imperative by the solemn voice of Vedic injunction. It is the indefeasible birth-right of every Brahman. It is his distinctive badge. It is his special privilege that he can address his Father in the words that his fathers used thousands of years ago and in the same tones. And what noble words they are, how redolent of love and reverence, humility and faith!

Is it then asking too much of him, if we call on him to remember his noble lineage, if we implore him, by all he holds scared, to discharge in an adequate manner a duty which he owes alike to himself and to his fathers? We ask not for a blind and undiscriminating admiration for everything that has come down to us from of old. All that we ask of him is to exercise his franchise as a thinking being and hold fast to that which is good. Is this then asking too much? We hope not, we fervently pray not.

G. A. NATESAN & CO., PRINTERS, ESPLANADE MADRAS.